To Ted:

Thanks ...
book, Te...
sheet, than...
an uninitiated become initiated
into the complexities of the
international law of the sea.

Dack VanderZwaag

Aug. 19/83

The Fish Feud

The Fish Feud

**The U.S. and Canadian
Boundary Dispute**

David L. VanderZwaag
Dalhousie Ocean
Studies Programme

LexingtonBooks
D.C. Heath and Company
Lexington, Massachusetts
Toronto

Library of Congress Cataloging in Publication Data

VanderZwaag, David L.
    The fish feud.

    Bibliography: p.
    Includes index.
    1. Fishery policy—United States. 2. Fishery policy—Canada.
3. Fishery management—United States. 4. Fishery management—Canada.
I. Title.
SH221.V36 1983   341.7'622'097   82-49322
ISBN 0-669-06611-7

Copyright © 1983 by D.C. Heath and Company

Published simultaneously in Canada

Printed in the United States of America

International Standard Book Number: 0-669-06611-7

Library of Congress Catalog Card Number: 82-49322

To Douglas M. Johnston

Contents

Figures

Preface

The United States-Canada relationship over the East Coast fisheries is in a state of divorce. Canadian fishermen are banned from fishing in U.S. waters. American fishermen are banned from fishing in Canadian waters. A fish feud has occurred in the disputed zone of Georges Bank. U.S. fishermen have harvested with little regulation, and Canadian fishermen·have operated under relaxed regulations. Although both countries have agreed to settle the boundary dispute before a Chamber of the International Court of Justice, American interests have refused to negotiate with Canada on an interim fisheries agreement, at least until the boundary is settled.

Once the boundary is settled, the potential for conflict will not abate. Fish stocks will not pledge allegiance to either country but will insist on dual citizenship and the right to transborder travel without restraint. Canadian fishermen could seek to vacuum the fish stocks while the fish are on Canadian holiday. American fishermen could seek to hoard the fish stocks while the fish are on American tour. Overfished and exhausted fish stocks could be the result.

How may Canada and the United States avoid such a situation? How should they cooperate over fishery management in the future? These are the questions this book attempts to answer. Chapter 1, after summarizing the geography and oceanography of the Gulf of Maine-Georges Bank region, reviews the distributions and landings of the major fish stocks and isolates those stocks with the greatest conflict potential. Chapter 2 explores the U.S. fisheries-management regime. Chapter 3 highlights the Canadian fisheries-management system. Chapter 4 analyzes the ill-fated East Coast Fisheries Agreement of 1979. Chapter 5 concludes by proposing future options for linking the Canadian and American fisheries-management systems.

Acknowledgments

The Dalhousie Ocean Studies Programme supported my research for this book through the generous award of a Dalhousie Ocean Studies Fellowship.

I am grateful to Professor Douglas M. Johnston for his patient supervision and wealth of creative ideas; to Norman Letalik and Peter Underwood, of the Dalhousie Ocean Studies Programme, for research suggestions; and to Douglas Marshall, executive director of the New England Fisheries Management Council, and Dr. R.D.S. MacDonald, Dr. G.M. Hare, and Dr. M.M. Sinclair of the Department of Fisheries and Oceans for reviewing selected chapters.

Numerous officials from the Department of Fisheries and Oceans, especially Greg Peacock, Nancy Dale, Richard Crouter, Dr. R.G. Halliday, and Bob Prier, gave their time and information. David Bollivar of National Sea Products Ltd. and Roger Stirling, executive director of Seafood Producers Association of Nova Scotia shared their industry points of view. And officials from the National Marine Fisheries Service in Gloucester, Massachusetts, clarified the federal role in fisheries management.

Professor Christian Wiktor and his staff at the Sir James Dunn Library at Dalhousie Law School provided librarianship services beyond the call of duty. Judy Reade at the Dalhousie Institute for Resource and Environmental Studies opened the doors to an excellent environmental library. My wife, Cindy Vander-Zwaag, prepared the illustrations in chapter 1. Ted McDorman, of the Dalhousie Ocean Studies Programme, indexed the book. Georgie Edgett typed this manuscript. I thank them all.

The Region and the Resource

The Region: A Geographic and Oceanographic Overview

The Gulf of Maine, with an average depth of about 490 feet and an area of about 36,000 square miles, is rectangular in shape.[1] Maine and New Brunswick form the top of the rectangle. The Bay of Fundy and Nova Scotia form the right side. New Hampsnire and Massachusetts border the left, and two underwater plateaus, Georges Bank and Browns Bank, protect the bottom from the open Atlantic (figure 1-1).

The gulf's dimensions are impressive. Its width is approximately 225 nautical miles from Cape Ann, Maine, to Cape Sable Island, Nova Scotia, and its length is 130 miles from Mount Desert Isle, Maine, to the northern edge of Georges Bank. The coastline from Cape Cod, Massachusetts to Nova Scotia, including all indented bays and tidal rivers, meanders for nearly 5,000 miles.[2]

Georges Bank, approximately 174 miles long and 93 miles wide, juts out like a thumb from the coast of Cape Cod.[3] The bank's depth varies from about 15 feet near the center to about 600 feet near the edges.[4] The bank's base and tip are demarcated by two deep channels. The Great South Channel separates the Bank from the U.S. East Coast shelf; the Northeast Channel separates the bank from the Scotian Shelf (figure 1-1).

Studies show Georges Bank to be one of the most-productive ocean areas in the world. The production of phytoplankton, the basic building block in the aquatic food chain, is three to five times higher than in other oceanic systems, with 400 to 500 grams of carbon per square meter compared with only 250 grams for Long Island Sound and 90 grams for the North Sea.[5] The bank boasts a standing crop of benthos (fixed or crawling organisms) such as scallops, sea cucumbers, lobsters, and quahogs, nearly 1.8 times more abundant than the Gulf of Maine and 1.3 times more abundant than the Scotian Shelf.[6] While also high in the production of pelagics (surface dwellers), such as herring, mackerel, and squid, the bank nourishes extremely large populations of demersals (bottom dwellers), such as cod, haddock, and flounder, estimated to be three to four times more productive than in the North Sea.[7] In fact, half of the sustainable yield of fisheries from the Gulf of Maine to Cape Hatteras may be attributable to the relatively small area of Georges Bank.[8]

Such biological enrichment depends on at least three ecological factors. First, the shallowness of Georges Bank allows excellent penetration of sunlight, a key element for phytoplankton to carry on photosynthesis. Second, a

1

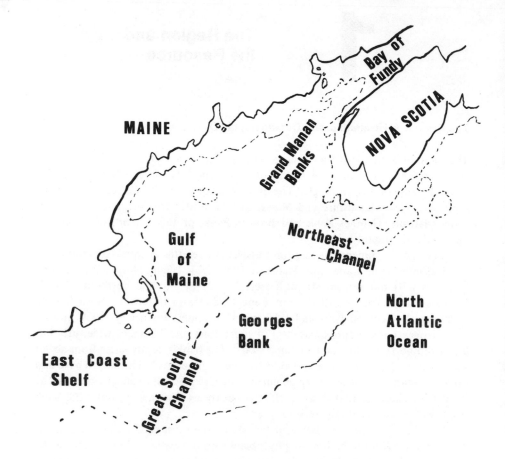

Source: Adapted from S. Apollonia, *The Gulf of Maine* 8 (1979). Used with permission.

Figure 1-1. Geography of the Gulf of Maine-Georges Bank

clockwise current or eddy around the bank combines with tidal currents, wind currents, and wave action to keep bottom nutrients well mixed in the water column. Third, upwellings from deeper water on the sides of the bank provide a lavish supply of additional nutrients from the ocean floor.[9]

Gulf of Maine waters, charged by nutrient-rich rivers such as the St. John and St. Croix and fed by an inflow of cold ocean water along the Scotian shelf and through the Northeast Channel, show a counterclockwise rotation.[10] Such a gyre may not only influence the migration of marine species but may also increase marine fertility by contributing to nutrient mixing.[11]

The Resource: Stock Distributions and Landings

Which fish stocks will cause future management conflicts between the United States and Canada is difficult to predict.[12] Much depends on future fishing efforts and regulatory actions of each country and on future ecological factors. Favorable mortality or recruitment rates for a particular stock could increase biomass and, in turn, satisfy national appetites. Unfavorable conditions could deplenish a stock and thereby tense national nerves. Much depends on future political rest or unrest of special-interest groups such as fishermen and processors. Nevertheless, some idea of the potentiality for conflict may be surmised from the litmus of stock distributions and landings. Common sense dictates that stocks with the greatest jurisdictional overlap and having the greatest economic importance should be more prone to sour international relations.

Stock distributions and landings can be examined under five major headings: species with high conflict potential regardless of the eventual boundary line; species with high conflict potential depending on the boundary; species with moderate conflict potential regardless of the boundary; species with moderate conflict potential depending on the boundary; and species with low conflict potential regardless of the boundary.

Two cautions are in order. First, the following distribution discussions and graphics should be treated as more impressionistic than photographic, for scientific knowledge is still very limited, and stock movements, varied by such factors as temperature, salinity, and current, are never constant.[13] Second, while hundreds of species frequent the North Atlantic and could be measured for conflict potential, this section will analyze only the major fish species in the Gulf of Maine-Georges Bank region.[14] Only the fifteen species important enough to have been specifically negotiated over in the ill-fated East Coast Fisheries Agreement of 1979 will be covered.[15]

Species with High Conflict Potential Regardless
of the Eventual Boundary Line

Herring (Clupea harengus): Although several dozen herring stocks may inhabit the northwest Atlantic, only three—the Georges Bank stock, the Gulf of Maine stock, and the Nova Scotia stock—appear to have major international conflict potential.[16] At least four conflict scenarios are possible (figure 1-2).

First, U.S. fishermen could snatch "Nova Scotia fish" in U.S. waters. Although the Nova Scotia herring stock appears to feed during the summer off southwest Nova Scotia and the Bay of Fundy mouth and to spawn in the autumn on Scotian shallows such as Lurchers Shoal, a proportion may migrate

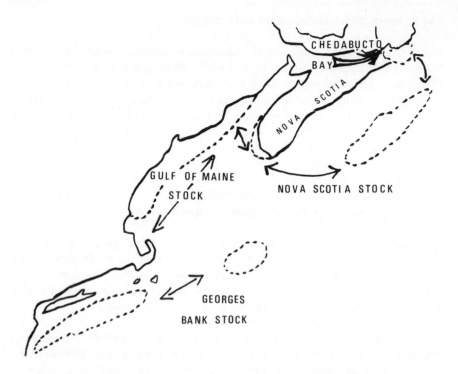

Source: Modified from G.M. Hare, "Atlas of the Major Atlantic Coast Fish and Invertebrate Resources Adjacent to the Canada-United States Boundary Areas," *Environment Canada Fisheries and Marine Service Tech. Rept. No. 61* 6 (1977)

Figure 1-2. Herring Distributions with Conflict Potential

and overwinter in the Gulf of Maine to Cape Cod area, while another proportion spends the season up north off the Chedabucto Bay region.[17]

Second, U.S. fishermen could overexploit "Canadian juveniles" while Canadian fishermen could overfish "U.S. juveniles," for juvenile herring, the foundation of the lucrative sardine industry, range up and down the Maine-New Brunswick coast.[18] Young herring could travel, however, as far north as St. Margaret's Bay (south-central Nova Scotia) and as far south as Massachusetts or Rhode Island.[19]

Third, if the boundary cuts across Georges Bank, U.S. fishermen could abduct "Canadian herring" on winter tour south of Cape Cod, or Canadian fishermen could kidnap "U.S. fish" during warm-weather spawning on Canadian beds. Georges Bank herring spawn on northern Georges Bank but apparently overwinter far to the west, south of Cape Cod.[20]

Fourth, if U.S. fishermen overprey on Gulf of Maine or Georges Bank adults, "Canadian juveniles" could suffer. Or if Canadian fishermen overharvest Nova Scotia adults, "U.S. juveniles" could falter. (The process could also be reversed; overfishing of juveniles could deplete parent stocks.) The Gulf of Maine-Bay of Fundy juvenile fishery may depend on larval drifts from Georges Bank adults, Gulf of Maine adults, and Nova Scotia adults.[21] Thus, a reduction of a parent stock could cause a corresponding reduction in the juvenile stock.

Atlantic herring is an important commercial species to both the United States and Canada. Only cod, haddock, lobster, scallops, and menhaden rank higher in the U.S. east coast fishery.[22] Only cod, lobster, and scallops rank higher in the Canadian fishery.[23]

Recent landing statistics show Canadian catches nearly double that of the United States in both weight and value. In 1979 Canadian fishermen landed 141,467 tons of Atlantic herring valued at $25.72 million, and in 1980 they landed 148,030 tons valued at $29.90 million.[24] The United States, meanwhile, averaged about 50,000 tons in 1977-1978 but increased the catch to 91,996 tons valued at $10.36 million in 1980.[25]

Atlantic herring appear to carry high potential for creating future management conflicts between the U.S. and Canada because of substantial stock overlaps and high commercial value.

Species with High Conflict Potential Depending on the Boundary

Cod (Gadus Morhua): Eight major cod complexes populate the offshore area from the Gulf of St. Lawrence south to North Carolina.[26] (See figure 1-3.) One stock, the Georges Bank stock, will certainly involve conflict potential if Canada wins a portion of Georges Bank for such cod concentrate on the bank's north-northeastern portion where any boundary would probably cause a substantial stock overlap.[27] Two cod stocks may contribute to at least a minor overlap, no matter where the line is drawn. The Georges Bank stock and the Browns Bank stock (in Canadian waters) show some mixing.[28] Four other stocks may contribute at least tangentially to the Georges-Brown overlap by virtue of mixing with either the Georges or Brown stocks. On the U.S. side, the southern New England and Middle Atlantic stocks intermingle extensively with the Georges Bank stock.[29] On the Canadian side, the Nova Scotia coastal stock complex and the Banquereau-Sable Island complex may mix to some extent with the Browns Bank stock.[30] Two stocks appear to be isolated from international conflict. The Gulf of Maine stock is concentrated on the western Gulf of Maine (U.S. waters) and shows only minimal interchange with the Georges Bank stock.[31] The southern Gulf of St. Lawrence stock prefers Canadian waters and limits its migrations between the Laurentian Channel and the Gulf of St. Lawrence.[32]

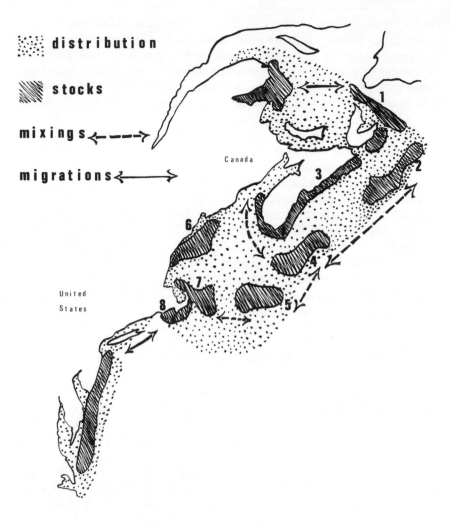

distribution

stocks

mixings ←--→

migrations ←→

Source: Modified from Hare, *supra* figure 1-2.
(1) Southern Gulf of St. Lawrence; (2) Banquereau Bank-Sable Island; (3) Nova Scotia Coastal; (4) Browns Bank; (5) Georges Bank; (6) Gulf of Maine; (7) Southern New England; and (8) Middle Atlantic.

Figure 1-3. Cod Distribution and Stock Structure

    Cod rank high in commercial value to both U.S. and Canadian fisheries. Only scallops, lobsters, and menhaden rank higher in importance to the New England fishery.[33] Only scallops and lobsters rank higher to the maritime provinces.[34] U.S. catches of Atlantic cod were 49,676 tons valued at $28.63 million in 1979 and 59,123 tons valued at $31.88 million in 1980.[35] Canadian catches were over two times higher in weight: 137,105 tons valued at $44 million in 1979 and 147,431 tons valued at $47.97 million in 1980.[36]

If the boundary is drawn across Georges Bank, conflict potential over Atlantic cod would probably be high because of four factors: substantial stock overlap, high commercial value, contrasting management schemes,[37] and possible market competition.[38] If the boundary is drawn through the Northeast Channel, conflict potential would probably be much lower and hinge on the amount of stock intermixing between Georges and Browns banks.

Haddock (Melanogrammus aeglefinus): At least eight haddock populations may inhabit the continental shelf from Newfoundland to southern New England (figure 1-4). Four of these stocks will clearly provoke no international management conflict. The western Newfoundland stock, the St. Pierre Bank stock, and the Grand Banks stock are all isolated from U.S. and Nova Scotia stocks by the deep Laurentian Channel.[39] The eastern Scotian Shelf stock appears isolated by the deep Emerald and LaHave Basins off Halifax and Lunenburg.[40] Four other stocks could, however, contribute to international conflict. The Georges Bank stock, concentrating on the eastern portion of the bank, would show a considerable jurisdictional overlap if the boundary eventually crosses Georges Bank.[41] The western Gulf of Maine stock (also referred to as the Jeffreys Ledge stock), regardless of the boundary line, would produce at least a minor overlap, since the gulf stock migrates northward into the Bay of Fundy (Canadian waters) during summer and returns south in winter.[42] A Nantucket Shoals stock could contribute to the overlap, since intermingling between Nantucket Shoals haddock and Gulf of Maine haddock obviously occurs.[43] The western Nova Scotia stock could also boost the international overlap, since some mixing with the Gulf of Maine stock is known to occur, although tagging studies have indicated that movement between the two stocks is not extensive.

Haddock is a highly prized commercial fishery to both the United States and Canada.[44] In 1979 and 1980, U.S. fishermen landed 20,941 tons of haddock valued at $17.71 million and 27,594 tons valued at $21.43 million, respectively.[45] In the same years Canadian Maritimers netted, respectively, 36,785 tons valued at $15.62 million and 57,195 tons valued at $27.21 million.[46]

If the boundary line crosses Georges Bank, conflict potential over haddock would probably be high due to four factors: substantial stock overlap, high commercial value, contrasting management schemes,[47] and market competition.[48] If the boundary crosses through the Northeast Channel and leaves the Georges Bank stock totally in U.S. hands, conflict potential would certainly be much less and depend on the extent of overlap in the Gulf of Maine-Bay of Fundy region, which appears to be minor.

Atlantic Sea Scallop (Placopecten magellanicus): Sea scallops are distributed

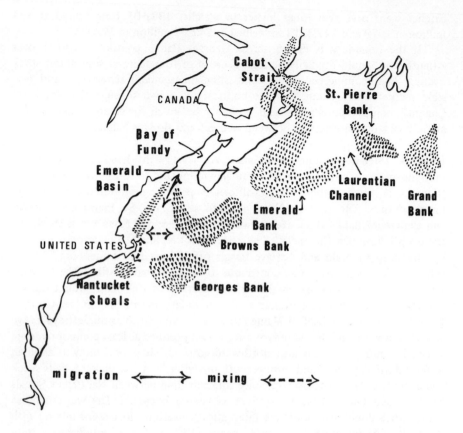

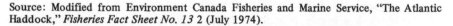

Source: Modified from Environment Canada Fisheries and Marine Service, "The Atlantic Haddock," *Fisheries Fact Sheet No. 13* 2 (July 1974).

Figure 1-4. Haddock Distribution in the Northwest Atlantic

along the Atlantic Coast from the Gulf of St. Lawrence south to Cape Hatteras (figure 1-5).[49] The greatest concentration is on Georges Bank, with four areas of the bank being most productive.[50] The northern edge is the greatest and most-consistent producer; the northeast peak and south channel are consistent but less productive; and the southeast part is sporadic but occasionally productive.[51]

Tagging studies suggest scallops are essentially nonmigratory.[52] Thus, regardless of the eventual boundary line, stock overlap should be negligible.[53]

Sea scallops are highly important to both U.S. and Canadian fishermen. Overall U.S. catches in 1979 and 1980 were 15,733 tons valued at $103.20 million and 14,376 tons valued at $110.43 million, respectively.[54] Overall Canadian catches in 1978 and 1979 were 120,596 tons valued at $63.48 million and 98,643 tons valued at $74.45 million, respectively.[55]

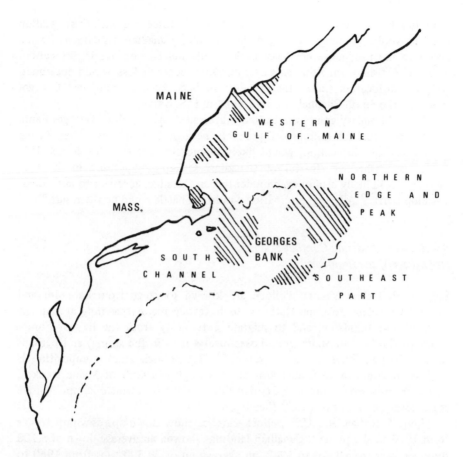

Source: New England Fishery Management Council, *Fishery Management Plan Final Environmental Impact Statement Regulatory Impact Review for Atlantic Sea Scallops (Placopecten magellanicus)* 4 (January 1982).

Figure 1-5. Sea Scallop Resources off the Northeast United States

National harvests from Georges Bank have shown great variations. Up to 1950 only New England fishermen took scallops from the bank. In 1951 Canadian boats initiated their first harvest, a mere 100 tons compared to a U.S. catch of 6,299 tons.[56] By 1961 the Canadian catch grew to 5,014 tons compared to a U.S. catch of 11,751 tons.[57] From 1961 to 1980, Canada's annual scallop landings were nearly double those of the United States. Canada averaged 6,969 tons compared to a U.S. figure of 3,924 tons.[58] In 1980 the United States again regained supremacy by landing 6,195 tons to Canada's 5,775.[59]

If the boundary grants Canada part of eastern Georges Bank, conflict potential for scallops will probably be low for three reasons. First, scallop overlap would probably be negligible. Second, Canadian fishermen, having access to the productive northeast peak, would not face economic dislocation. Third, U.S. fishermen, although suffering some economic loss, would not undergo great dislocation since other productive beds—such as southeast Georges Bank and the South Channel—would still be in U.S. waters.

If the boundary grants the United States all or nearly all of Georges Bank, conflict potential for scallops will probably be high. Canadian fishermen, facing great economic dislocation, would likely clamor for access rights to the U.S. zone. U.S. fishermen, fearful of Canadian scallop competition in the U.S. market, would likely clamor even louder to ban Canadian access or to implement a scallop tariff.[60] A heated international political battle could be the result.[61]

Species with Moderate Conflict Potential
Regardless of the Boundary

Pollock (Pollachius virens): Pollock are known to range from Labrador and western Greenland to Cape Hatteras, to have one major spawning area in the western Gulf of Maine, and to migrate extensively from the Bay of Fundy south to the Gulf of Maine and Massachusetts Bay (in the spring) and perhaps to the Scotian Shelf (in late autumn).[62] But pollock stock composition is unclear. It could range from a four-stock complex—a Gulf of Maine stock, a Bay of Fundy stock, and two Scotian Shelf stocks—to a single comprehensive stock covering the entire area.[63] (See figure 1-6.)

Both Canadian and U.S. pollock catches show down-up, down-up trends from 1920 to the present. Canadian landings showed an average down of 5,100 tons per year from 1920 to 1942, an average up of 29,300 tons from 1960 to 1964, a down of 10,800 tons in 1970, and an average up of 25,600 tons from 1973 to 1978.[64] In 1979 Canada continued on the up trend by landing 34,422 tons of pollock valued at $6.98 million.[65] U.S. landings, meanwhile, showed an average down of 3,600 tons from 1920 to 1929, an average up of 13,400 tons from 1935 to 1960, and an average down of 3,300 tons in 1967-1968.[66] Recent U.S. landings demonstrate an upward trend, with 17.773 tons valued at $6.66 million caught in 1979 and 19,826 tons valued at $7.17 million caught in 1980.[67]

Recent U.S. and Canadian pollock catches may be much lower than the actual statistics, for fishermen in both countries may have misreported haddock as pollock in order to bypass stringent haddock quotas.[68]

The pollock fishery includes factors both high and low in conflict potential. The extensive migrations of pollock between U.S. and Canadian waters and the previous ability of the stock(s) to contribute to international hostility would indicate a high conflict potential. The species' lack of great economic

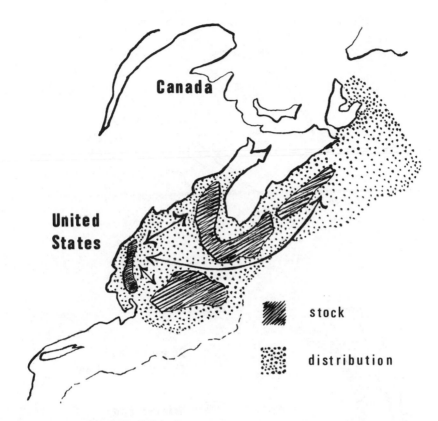

Source: Hare, *supra* figure 1-2, at 3.

Figure 1-6 Pollock Distribution and Stock Structure

importance and the species' lack of present regulation would suggest a low conflict potential. By an averaging process, then. at least a moderate conflict rating would seem to be justified.[69]

Illex Squid (Illex illecebrosus): *Illex illecebrosus*, also called the short-finned squid, ranges from Greenland to Florida and is relatively abundant between Nova Scotia and New Jersey (figure 1-7).[70] Knowledge of stock structure is still cloaked in mystery, for although Illex are known to move onto the continental shelf during summer and fall—for example, moving onto the Scotian Shelf from about April through November and onto the Grand Banks from about May to November—the origin of such influx is open to question.[71]

At least two major possibilities exist. U.S. squid and Canadian squid, particularly those on the Scotian Shelf, could be part of the same stock complex, which perhaps spawns off the New England-Middle Atlantic coast during

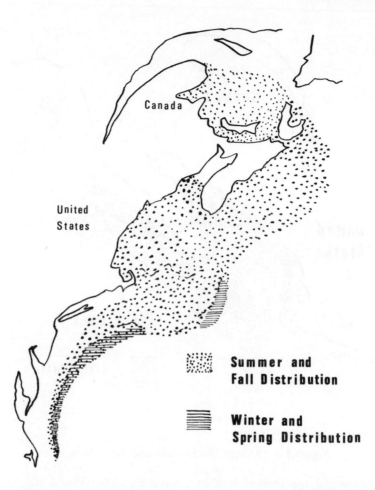

Canada

United
States

::::: **Summer and
Fall Distribution**

≡ **Winter and
Spring Distribution**

Source: From U.S. Department of State, *Draft Environmental Impact Statement on the Agreement between the United States and Canada on East Coast Fishery Resources* 71 (April 1980).

Figure 1-7. Illex Squid Distribution

winter.[72] Or Canadian squid could be a separate stock or stocks with independent spawning areas such as the Gulf Stream or the offshore depths.[73] Given the possibility, then, of an Illex migration between U.S. and Canadian waters, a substantial overlap could occur regardless of the final boundary line.[74]

Illex squid has traditionally been a species of low commercial importance to the United States and Canada.[75] For example, from 1975 to 1978 the United

States harvested an average of 916 tons per year, while Canada netted a still rather meager average of 23,557 tons per year.[76]

Recent statistics, however, show a shift toward higher commercial value. In 1979 the United States landed about 3,300 tons, valued at approximately $2.10 million, and Canada's harvest soared to near 123,450 tons, valued at $30.34 million.[77]

Because of the possibility of a substantial stock overlap and growing commercial importance, Illex's conflict potential should be rated as at least moderate.

Species with Moderate Conflict Potential
Depending on the Boundary

Lobster (Homarus americanus): American lobster ranges from Labrador to Cape Hatteras.[78] While studies of lobster movements are not conclusive, certain patterns seem to be surfacing.[79] Inshore lobsters are generally nonmigratory in contrast to offshore lobsters, which may undergo extensive migrations.[80] Offshore lobsters, apparently seeking optimal temperatures, tend to creep inshore toward warming nearshore waters in the spring and summer and to crawl offshore as the coastal waters cool in the fall.[81] (See figure 1-8.)

Gulf of Maine lobsters tend to concentrate along the coast from north of Cape Cod to the Bay of Fundy. Georges Bank lobsters appear to concentrate along the south-southeastern edge in winter, with summer concentrations over the southwestern and northeastern regions.

If the boundary line crosses Georges Bank, at least some minor stock overlap would probably occur. The extent of the overlap is impossible to predict with any certainty, however, since tagging studies are so few and often conflicting.

Lobster has ranked number two in commercial value to both New Englanders and Maritimers.[82] Overall U.S. catches in 1979 and 1980 were 18,592 tons valued at $72.30 million and 18,476 tons valued at $75.23 million, respectively.[83] Overall Canadian harvests have tended to be slightly higher, with 21,141 tons valued at $75.59 million landed in 1978 and 23,783 tons valued at $83.30 million landed in 1979.[84]

Georges Bank catches, however, have been comparatively moderate. In 1977 the United States took 1,350 tons on Georges Bank, while Canada cornered 268 tons.[85] In 1978 the United States caught 1,369 tons compared to Canada's 297 tons.[86]

If the boundary crosses Georges Bank, lobster could store moderate conflict potential based on two factors: a traditionally moderate harvest of Georges Bank lobsters and at least a minor population overlap.

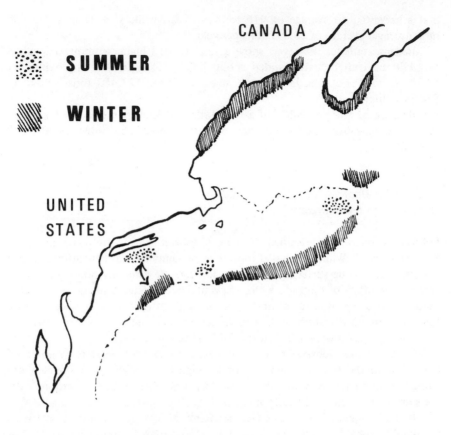

Figure 1-8. Lobster Concentrations in the Gulf of Maine-Georges Bank

*Species with Low Conflict Potential Regardless
of the Boundary Line*

Argentine (Argentina Silus): While detailed assessments are lacking, argentine are known to range in deep waters of the Scotian Shelf southward to Georges Bank (figure 1-9).[87] Their largest gatherings occur along the edge of the Scotian Shelf, particularly near Browns Bank off southwest Nova Scotia.[88] Their Georges Bank habitation is limited to the bank's eastern edge.[89] Although some stock overlap would occur regardless of the eventual boundary location, such overlap will probably be localized and minimal since mixing among adjacent stock units appears limited.[90]

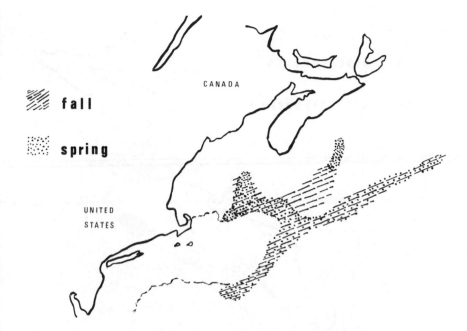

fall

spring

CANADA

UNITED
STATES

Source: From *Draft Environmental Impact Statement, supra* figure 1-7, at 57.

Figure 1-9. Argentine Distribution

Argentine fishing in the northwest Atlantic has been almost totally a foreign affair.[91] In fact, the United States does not even issue individual statistics for argentine catches but relegates any U.S. catches to the catch-all category "other finfish."[92] Canadian statistics also do not list any domestic argentine catches, but only note cooperative arrangements with foreign vessels.[93]

Given the lack of a domestic fishery and the lack of a major stock overlap, argentine's conflict potential appears to be low.

Cusk (Brosme brosme): Cusk range in moderately deep waters from the Strait of Belle Isle and Newfoundland Grand Banks south to Cape Cod, with the center of abundance apparently the Scotian Shelf (figure 1-10).[94] In the boundary area, cusk roam on the northern and southern edges of Georges Bank in spring and across the Gulf of Maine in fall.[95] Since cusk tend to be solitary fish and not particularly abundant, stock overlap would probably be minor regardless of the eventual boundary.[96]

Commercial importance of cusk to the United States and Canada has been relatively low. U.S. catches in 1979 and 1980 were a mere 1,868 tons valued at $792,000 and 2,149 tons valued at $872,000, respectively.[97] Canadian catches

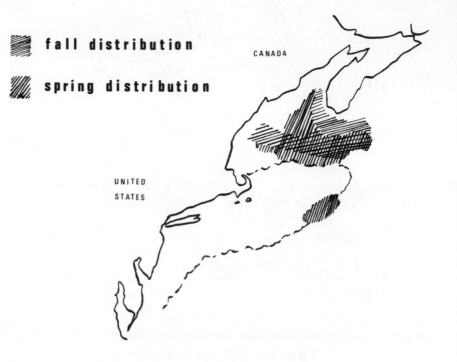

Source: *Draft Environmental Impact Statement, supra* figure 1-7, at 59.

Figure 1-10. Cusk Distribution in the Boundary Area

in 1978 and 1979 were, respectively, 5,855 tons valued at $1.43 million and 5,413 tons valued at $1.74 million.[98]

Cusk conflict potential appears to be low for two reasons: low commercial importance and limited stock overlap.

Redfish (Sebastes marinus): Redfish, also called ocean perch, range in deep waters from the coast of Greenland to Georges Bank (figure 1-11).[99] Although distributed around the deep fringes of Georges Bank, redfish concentrate in the central Gulf of Maine.[100] Tagging studies and knowledge of stock structure are lacking, but trawling surveys suggest redfish are relatively stationary.[101] Thus, although the boundary line is bound to cut across the redfish stock in the Gulf of Maine, stock migration probably will be minor at most.

Redfish is of moderate commercial importance to both the United States and Canada.[102] U.S. catches in 1979 and 1980 were 17,020 tons valued at $7.16 million and 12,102 tons valued at $5.55 million, respectively.[103] Canadian

SPRING
   DISTRIBUTION

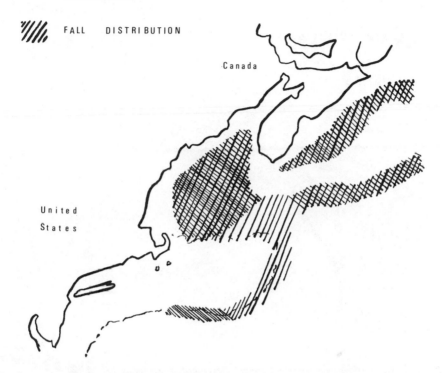

Source: From *Draft Environmental Impact Statement, supra* figure 1-7, at 68.

Figure 1-11. Redfish Distribution and Concentration

catches have been two to three times as high in value, with 84,949 tons valued at $13.07 million landed in 1978 and 88,875 tons valued at $15.41 million landed in 1979.[104] However, Canadian catches from the Gulf of Maine-Georges Bank region have been low, averaging 150 tons per year from 1975 to 1978.[105]

Redfish's conflict potential would appear to be low for two reasons: a minor stock overlap and a traditionally low Canadian catch in the Gulf of Maine-Georges Bank region.

Silver Hake (Merluccius bilinearis): Other than the known general distribution from the Grand Banks to South Carolina, knowledge of silver hake distribution is still rather sparse (figure 1-12).[106] In Canadian waters, two concentrations occur: an eastern concentration, appearing to be a separate stock, along the Canso and Sable Island Banks, and a western concentration, along the Browns-

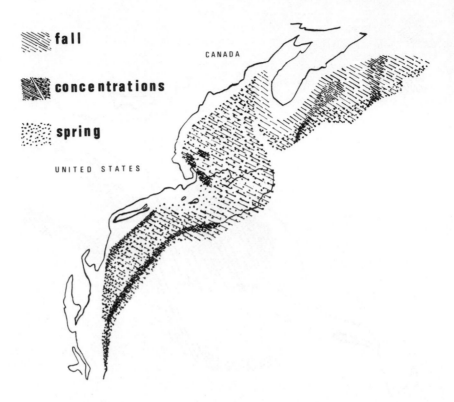

Source: From *Draft Environmental Impact Statement, supra* figure 1-7, at 62.

Figure 1-12. Silver Hake Distribution and Concentration

LaHave-Emerald Basin area whose discreteness is unknown.[107] In U.S. waters, three stocks are usually distinguished: the Gulf of Maine stock, the Georges Bank stock, and the southern New England-Middle Atlantic stock.[108] The Gulf of Maine and Georges Bank stocks, however, may be a single population, and the southern New England-Middle Atlantic stock may be two separate stocks.[109]

If the U.S. boundary claim prevails, the boundary line will cut only the Gulf of Maine stock, but if the Canadian claim prevails, the boundary line will also cut across the Georges Bank stock. In either case, however, the overlap would probably be minor for two reasons. First, tagging studies have indicated a lack of significant movement of silver hake from one area to another.[110] Second, the greatest silver hake concentrations will probably occur west of any line.

It is difficult to piece together a clear picture of silver hake's commercial importance since recent statistics are so sketchy. U.S. Department of Commerce statistics list only commercial catches for Pacific red and white hakes.[111] The most-recent Canadian Annual Statistical Review gives only a combined catch for all hake species.[112]

Nevertheless, other sources do allow the construction of a mosaic. Canadian fishermen traditionally have not fished in U.S. waters.[113] For example, Canadian silver hake catches from Georges Bank averaged less than 1 ton per year with yearly values less than a thousand dollars from 1970 to 1977.[114] Canadian fishermen have hardly fished for silver hake in their own waters. In 1978 Canadian fishermen landed only 110 tons compared to foreign catches of 53,131 tons.[115] In 1979 Canadian fishermen reportedly caught no silver hake compared to foreign catches of 57,099 tons.[116] U.S. fishermen have not traditionally fished for silver hake in Canadian waters, and although enjoying moderately high catches from U.S. waters from 1955 through 1964, U.S. fishermen have seen their catches plummet because of poor markets and stock decline.[117] For example, U.S. catches from Georges Bank averaged only 3,899 tons per year from 1970 to 1971.[118] Values of the 1976 and 1977 catches were only $664,000 and $705,000, respectively.[119] Catches from the Gulf of Maine averaged only 8,708 tons from 1971 through 1978.[120] Thus, silver hake presents a picture of low commercial value.

Conflict potential of silver hake appears to be low for two reasons: low commercial importance and nonmigratory behavior.

Red Hake (Urophycis chuss): Red hake are found along the continental shelf from the Grand Banks of Newfoundland south to Virginia (figure 1-13).[121] Although the exact stock structure is unknown, red hake are assumed to consist of three major stocks: the Gulf of Maine stock, the Georges Bank stock, and a southern New England-Middle Atlantic stock.[122] The greatest concentration of red hake occurs along the south-southwest edge of Georges Bank.[123]

If the boundary crosses Georges Bank, the greatest concentration of red hake would occur on the U.S. side. Regardless of the boundary, stock overlap would occur in the Gulf of Maine. Such overlaps would probably be minor due to hake's rather stationary behavior.[124]

Red hake has been a species of low commercial importance to both the United States and Canada. U.S. catches from 1951 to 1974 averaged only 1,659 tons per year valued at $55,000 per year.[125] In 1979 and 1980, U.S. harvests were still rather low, with 3,520 tons valued at $953,000 and 2,799 tons valued at $677,000 respectively.[126] Canada's combined catch of all hake species amounted to only 12,323 tons valued at $2.15 million in 1978 and 14,312 tons valued at $2.67 million in 1979.[127] Canadian harvests of red hake from the boundary area have been almost negligible. For example, from 1965 to 1969, Canada averaged a take of only 8.8 tons per year from Georges Bank.[128] From 1970 to 1978 that take dropped to zero.[129] In 1979 Canada upped the catch from Georges Bank, but only to 331 tons.[130]

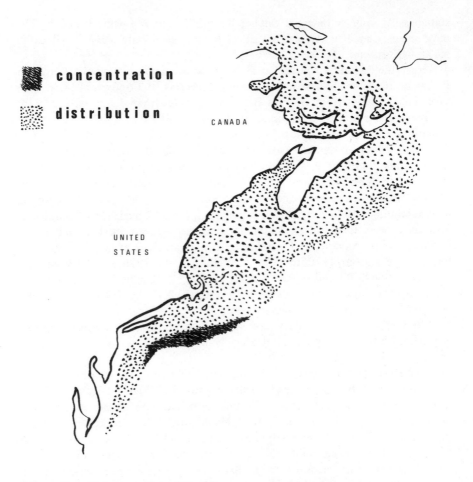

Source: From Hare, *supra* figure 1-2, at 4.

Figure 1-13. Red Hake Distribution and Concentration

Given the low commercial importance and the minor stock overlap, conflict potential for red hake appears to be low.

White Hake (Urophycis tenuis): The stock structure of white hake is unknown.[131] White hake are known to range along the Atlantic coast from the Gulf of St. Lawrence south to Virginia and North Carolina.[132] (See figure 1-14.) While common in the Gulf of Maine and on Georges Bank, concentrations appear to occur in the Gulf of St. Lawrence, along the Laurentian Channel, and at the Bay of Fundy mouth.[133] Since white hake are relatively stationary like their cousins, overlap would probably be minor regardless of the boundary line.[134]

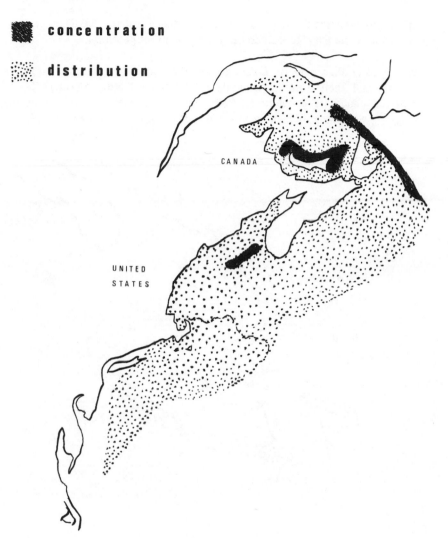

concentration

distribution

CANADA

UNITED
STATES

Source: From Hare, *supra* figure 1-2, at 4.

Figure 1-14. White Hake Distribution and Concentration

White hake has been a species of low commercial importance to both the United States and Canada. U.S. catches from 1975 to 1977 averaged 3,286 tons (per year) and have increased only slightly since then.[135] In 1978 the U.S. catch was 5,455 tons valued at $1.70 million; in 1979 the catch dipped to 4,441 tons valued at $1.47 million; and in 1980 the catch rose again to 5,214 tons valued at $1.74 million.[136] Canadian harvests have averaged about 20 percent less since 1967.[137]

Given the relatively low commercial importance and the relatively stationary behavior, white hake appears to carry a low conflict potential.

Loligo Squid (Loligo pealei): *Loligo pealei*, the long-finned squid, ranges over
the continental shelf from Nova Scotia to the Gulf of Mexico (figure 1-15).
Commercial quantities concentrate from southeastern Georges Bank to Cape
Hatteras.[138] Spawning, which occurs from May through September, centers

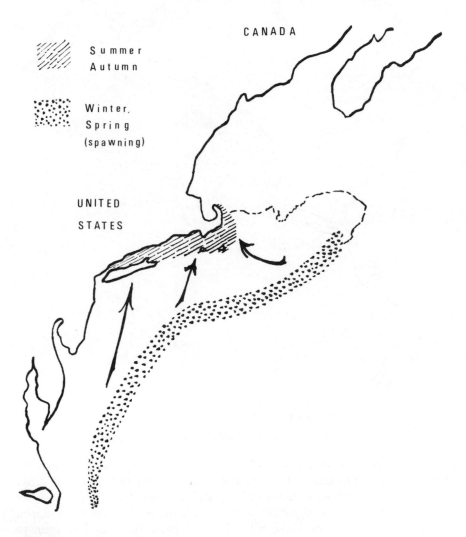

Source: From Hare, *supra* figure 1-2, at 7.

Figure 1-15. Loligo Squid Distribution

from Long Island to Cape Cod.[139] If the boundary crosses Georges Bank, a stock overlap would probably occur since Loligo in Canadian waters could undergo inshore migrations into shallow U.S. waters during summer and autumn. However, since Loligo would be concentrated primarily in U.S. territory, the overlap would probably not be substantial.

Loligo is not a commercially important species.[140] Since it is mainly a southern dweller, Canadian landings have been almost negligible.[141] U.S. landings were only 21 tons in 1975, 1,355 tons in 1976, 1,625 tons in 1977, and down to 741 tons in 1978.[142]

Given the low commercial value and lack of a major stock overlap, conflict potential for Loligo squid should be low regardless of the boundary.

Mackerel (Scomber scombrus): The scientific knowledge of mackerel distributions is a mixture of certainty and uncertainty. It is known that mackerel range broadly along the Atlantic coast from Labrador south to Cape Hatteras (figure 1-16).[143] There are two separate contingents: southern and northern. The southern contingent spawns from Long Island to Cape Cod, and the northern contingent spawns in the Gulf of St. Lawrence.[144] But it remains unclear whether the southern and northern contingents are one stock with major interbreeding but two migratory components or two stocks, with little interbreeding.[145] Details of the northern contingent's fall migration to the south and overwintering distribution are sparse.[146] The northern contingent appears to overwinter in the offshore waters from Hudson Canyon to Sable Island, while the southern contingent appears to bask offshore farther south, from Long Island to Chesapeake Bay.[147] The two contingents appear to intermix twice a year: in spring and in fall when their northerly and southerly migrations overlap.[148]

Pre-1950 catch statistics for Atlantic mackerel show great variations.[149] U.S. commercial landings range from a low of 306 tons in 1814 to a high of 89,640 tons in 1884. Canadian landings ranged from 3,490 tons in 1910 to 28,659 tons in 1879.[150]

From 1876 to 1949, the United States dominated the mackerel fishery. It led Canada in yearly catches fifty-seven times while Canada outfished the United States sixteen times and tied the United States once.

From 1950 to the present, Canada has clearly dominated, with an average yearly catch of approximately 14,300 tons compared to a U.S. commercial average of about 3,300 tons. Canadian mackerel landings in 1979 were 15,427 tons valued at $3.23 million. In 1980 catches fell slightly to 14,750 tons valued at $3.17 million.[151] U.S. commercial landings in 1979 were only 2,230 tons valued at $1.05 million and in 1980 were 2,955 tons valued at a mere $816,000.[152] Estimated U.S. recreational catches have averaged 1,820 tons per year.[153]

Although U.S. mackerel may be caught by Canadian fishermen all the way

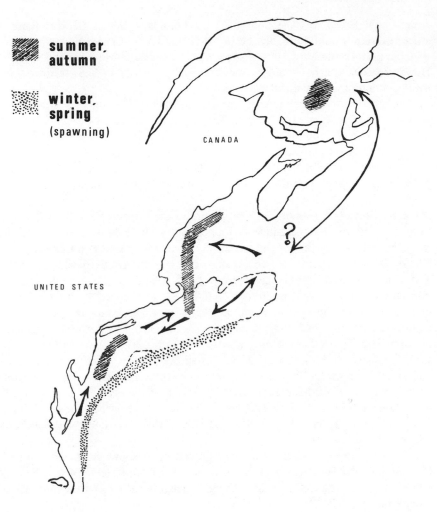

Source: From Hare, *supra* figure 1-2, at 6.

Figure 1-16. Mackerel Concentrations and Migrations

to Labrador and Canadian mackerel may be caught by U.S. fishermen all the way to North Carolina, conflict potential will probably still remain low due to low commercial importance. Mackerel continues to be a rather underutilized species for both countries. Although the United States set a commercial quota of 5,512 tons for the 1979-1980 fishing year, U.S. fishermen landed only around 3,000 tons.[154] Although Canadian scientists suggest a possible total allowable catch of over 100,000 tons per year, Canadian fishermen caught only approximately 30,000 tons in 1982.[155] Thus, mackerel is under no quota management.

If both countries greatly increase commercial or recreational harvests, however, conflict potential will likely turn high due to substantial stock overlap and differing management strategies. The United States would probably favor low mackerel quotas to ensure sportsmen a catch of older and fatter fish; Canada would probably favor high quotas to ensure commercial fishermen abundant harvests of younger, slimmer fish.[156]

Conclusion

One species, Atlantic herring, carries high conflict potential regardless of the boundary line. Two species, cod and haddock, have high conflict potential, which could become serious if the boundary crosses Georges Bank. One species, sea scallops, will bear high conflict potential if the United States wins all or nearly all of Georges Bank. Two species, pollock and Illex squid, carry moderate conflict potential regardless of the boundary. One species, American lobster, will store moderate conflict potential if the boundary slices Georges Bank. The eight remaining species—argentine, cusk, redfish, the three hakes, Loligo squid, and mackerel—have only a low potential for causing management conflict, regardless of the boundary line.

Notes

1. S. Apollonio, *The Gulf of Maine* 7 (1979).

2. *Id.* at 9.

3. U.S. Dept. of the Interior, *Final Environmental Statement, Proposed 1977 Outer Continental Shelf Oil & Gas Lease Sale Offshore the North Atlantic States, OCS Sale No. 42* 116 (1977).

4. C. Griscom, "Description of Georges Bank," in *Managing Our Georges Bank Resources* 1 (Proceedings from a Regional Forum Held at the University of Rhode Island, September 6-7, 1979).

5. E.B. Cohen, M.D. Grosslein, and M.P. Sissenwine, *An Energy Budget of Georges Bank* 4 (Presented at a Workshop on Multispecies Approaches to Fisheries Management, St. John's, Newfoundland, November 26-30, 1979).

6. Griscom, *supra* note 4, at 2.

7. Cohen et al., *supra* note 5, at 17-18.

8. G. McLeod and J. Prescott (eds.), *Georges Bank—Past, Present and Future of a Marine Environment* 4 (1982) [hereinafter referred to as Georges Bank—Past, Present and Future].

9. E.B. Cohen and W.R. Wright, *Primary Productivity on Georges Bank with an Explanation of Why It Is So High,* Northeast Fisheries Center, Lab. Ref. No. 79-53 (November 1979).

10. For charts of the seasonal current patterns in the Gulf of Maine, see W. Gusey, *The Fish and Wildlife Resources of the Georges Bank Region* 235-238 (1977).

11. For example, lobsters are believed to migrate with the counterclockwise current along the Maine coast. *See* J. Krouse, "Movement, Growth and Mortality of American Lobsters, Homarus americanus, Tagged Along the Coast of Maine," *NOAA Tech. Rept. NMFS SSRF-747,* pp. 7-8 (September 1981); D. Merriman, "The History of Georges Bank", in *Georges Bank—Past, Present and Future, supra* note 8, at 19.

12. Fish resources can be discussed in terms of species and stocks. A stock is a component of a species; it is essentially resident in a particular area with little interbreeding with stocks of the same species from other areas. B. Brown, *The Status of the Fishery Resources on Georges Bank,* Northeast Fisheries Center, Lab. Ref. No. 80-10 (November 1979).

13. D.J. Scarratt, "Biological Resources of the Bay of Fundy-Gulf of Maine System," in *Fundy Tidal Power and the Environment* 131-132 (January 1977).

14. For a general discussion of the hundreds of fish species, *see* H. Bigelow and W. Schroeder, "Fishes of the Gulf of Maine," 53 *U.S. Fish & Wildlife Serv. Bull.* 1-577 (1953).

15. The fifteen species covered by the agreement were: mackerel, pollock, cusk, northern lobster, Atlantic herring, scallops, Atlantic cod, haddock, silver hake, red hake, Atlantic argentine, white hake, redfish, Illex squid, and Loligo squid. For the text of the East Coast Fisheries Agreement, *see* U.S. Dept. of State, *Draft Environmental Impact Statement on the Agreement between the United States and Canada on East Coast Fisheries Resources Appendices,* Appendix 1 (March 1980) [hereinafter referred to as Draft Environmental Statement Appendices].

16. T.D. Iles and M. Sinclair, "Atlantic Herring: Stock Discreteness and Abundance," 215 *Science* 627 (February 5, 1982).

17. M. Sinclair and T.D. Iles, "Adult Herring Feeding Area off S.W. Nova Scotia" (Unpublished manuscript, Dept. Fisheries and Oceans, Halifax, 1980); W.T. Stobo, J.A. Moores, and J.J. Maguire, "The Herring and Mackerel Resources on the East Coast" *Background Paper for the East Coast Herring and Mackerel Seminar* 10 (February 17-19, 1981). *Also see* Fishery Management Plan for the Atlantic Herring Fishery of the Northwest Atlantic, 43 Fed. Reg. 60507 (December 28, 1978).

18. J.B. Colton, "The Enigma of Georges Bank Spawning," 6 *Limnology and Oceanography* 280, 290 (1961).

19. M. Sinclair, T.D. Iles, and W. Sutcliffe, "Herring Distributions within the Scotian Shelf-Gulf of Maine Area in Relation to Oceanographic Features" (Paper presented to the Symposium on Biological Productivity of Continental Shelves in the Temperate Zone of the North Atlantic 5, Kiel, Germany, March

2-5, 1982); Draft Environmental Statement Appendices, *supra* note 15, at 105.

20. G.M. Hare, "Atlas of the Major Atlantic Coast Fish and Invertebrate Resources Adjacent to the Canada-United States Boundary Areas," *Environment Canada Fisheries and Marine Service Tech. Rept. No. 61* 6 (1977). An update of this atlas should be published after the boundary litigation is completed. Personal communication, Department of Fisheries and Oceans official.

21. That all three stocks contribute to the juvenile fishery and the extent of such contributions is open to question, however. *See* H.C. Boyer et al., "Seasonal Distribution and Growth of Larval Herring (Clupea Harengus L.) in the Georges Bank-Gulf of Maine Area from 1962 to 1970" 35 *J. Int'l Council Explor. Sea* 36-51 (June 1973).

It is also open to question how seriously a reduction of adult stocks affects the juvenile fishery. Other stock larvae or favorable environmental conditions could offset a parental loss. *See* R.G. Lough and G.R. Bolz, "Abundance of Sea Herring (Clupea harengus L.) Larvae in Relation to Spawning Stock Size and Recruitment for the Gulf of Maine and Georges Bank, 1968-1978," Northeast Fisheries Center, Lab. Ref. No. 79-50 (November 1979), and A. Sinclair, M. Sinclair, and T.D. Illes, "An Analysis of Some Biological Characteristics of the 4X Juvenile-Herring Fishery," *Proceedings of the Nova Scotia Institute of Science*, vol. 31, pt. 2 (Halifax, 1981).

22. U.S. Dept. of Commerce, *Fisheries of the United States, 1980* 8-11 (April 1981) [hereinafter referred to as Fisheries of the United States, 1980].

23. Dept. of Fisheries and Oceans, *Canadian Fisheries Annual Statistical Review* 47 (Vol. 12, 1979) [hereinafter referred to as Canadian Annual Statistical Review, 1979].

24. Catch figures are limited to Nova Scotia, New Brunswick, and Prince Edward Island. Dept. of Fisheries and Oceans, *Annual Report 1980 Maritimes Region* 1 (1980) [hereinafter referred to as Maritimes Annual Report, 1980].

25. National Marine Fisheries Service, "Summary of Stock Assessments," Northeast Fisheries Center, Lab. Ref. No. 79-41, 14 (September 1979) [hereinafter referred to as Summary of Stock Assessments]. Fisheries of the United States, 1980, *supra* note 22, at 8.

26. Hare, *supra* note 20, at 1.

27. Gusey, *supra* note 10, at 366-367.

28. Hare, *supra* note 20, at 1. The major movement appears to be from Georges Bank to Browns Bank, with only minor movement in the opposite direction. Draft Environmental Statement Appendices, *supra* note 15, at 96. Given this mixing, it is debatable whether cod should be classified in category A (high conflict potential regardless of the boundary) or category B (high conflict potential depending on the boundary).

29. F.M. Serchuck, P.W. Wood, Jr., and D.M. Freid, "Current Assessment and Status of the Georges Bank and Gulf of Maine Cod Stocks,"

Northeast Fisheries Center, Lab. Ref. No. 80-07, 1 (February 1980) [herein-
after referred to as Cod Assessment].

30. Hare, *supra* note 20, at 1.

31. Cod Assessment, *supra* note 29, at 1.

32. Hare, *supra* note 20, at 1.

33. Fisheries of the U.S., 1980, *supra* note 22, at 8-11.

34. Maritime Annual Report, 1980, *supra* note 24, at 1.

35. Fisheries of the U.S., 1980, *supra* note 22, at 1.

36. Figures are limited to Nova Scotia, New Brunswick, and Prince
Edward Island. Maritime Annual Report 1980, *supra* note 24, at 1.

37. The United States is managing cod under an interim groundfish plan
with regulation limited to spawning area closures, mesh size (five and a half
inches), and fish size (seventeen inches). New England Fishery Management
Council, *Interim Fishery Management Plan for Atlantic Groundfish* (Sept. 30,
1981) [hereinafter referred to as Interim Groundfish Plan]. For the actual
groundfish regulations, *see* 47 Fed. Reg. 13357 (March 30, 1982), 50 C.F.R.
§651 (1982). Canada, meanwhile, has been managing cod with quotas and
closures. Dept. Fisheries and Oceans, Atlantic Groundfish Management Plan
1980 (Amended April 15, 1980) [hereinafter referred to as Atlantic Groundfish Plan].

U.S. cod regulations may, however, change in the future. The New England
Council is working on an Atlantic demersal finfish plan, which would encompass a multispecies management regime. That is, cod, haddock, yellowtail
flounder, silver hake, red hake, white hake, ocean perch, and pollock, would be
managed as a unit. Interim Groundfish Plan, at 45.

38. In 1980 the United States imported 80,209 tons of cod blocks or
slabs valued at $156.71 million and 65,706 tons of cod fillets valued at
$163.99 million. A large proportion of these imports were of Canadian origin.
Fisheries of the U.S., 1980, *supra* note 22, at 54.

39. Environment Canada Fisheries and Marine Service, "The Atlantic
Haddock," *Fisheries Fact Sheet No. 13* 2 (July 1974).

40. *Id.*

41. The Georges Bank stock appears to be relatively isolated from other
haddock stocks. S.H. Clark and W.J. Overholtz, "Review and Assessment of the
Georges Bank and Gulf of Maine Haddock Fishery," Northeast Fisheries Center,
Lab. Ref. No. 79-05, 8 (January 1979) [hereinafter referred to as Haddock
Assessment].

42. Hare, *supra* note 20, at 2. Given this overlap, it is debatable whether
haddock should be classified in category A (high conflict potential regardless of
the boundary) or category B (high conflict potential depending on the
boundary).

43. Haddock Assessment, *supra* note 41, at 9.

44. For a historical review of haddock catches on Georges Bank and in the Gulf of Maine, *see* S.H. Clark and R.J. Essig, "Georges Bank and Gulf of Maine Haddock Assessment Update" Northeast Fisheries Center, Lab. Ref. No. 80-06 (February 1980)

45. Fisheries of the U.S., 1980, *supra* note 22, at 1.

46. Maritimes Annual Report, 1980, *supra* note 24, at 1.

47. The United States is currently managing haddock under an interim plan with regulations limited to spawning area closures, mesh size (five and a half inches), and fish size (seventeen inches). Interim Groundfish Plan, *supra* note 37, at i. Canada invokes quotas and season closures. Atlantic Groundfish Plan, *supra* note 37, at 9-11.

48. In 1980 the United States imported 15,640 tons of haddock blocks and slabs valued at $36.16 million and 25,588 tons of haddock fillets valued at $58.33 million. A large proportion of these imports were from Canada. Fisheries of the U.S., 1980, *supra* note 22, at 54.

49. Draft Environmental Statement Appendices, *supra* note 15, at 115.

50. Hare, *supra* note 20, at 8.

51. New England Fishery Management Council, *Fishery Management Plan Final Environmental Impact Statement Regulatory Impact Review for Atlantic Sea Scallops (Placopecten magellanicus)* 4 (January 1982) [hereinafter referred to as Scallop Management Plan].

52. In a recent study, most scallops were recaptured within two to five miles of release. *See* J.A. Posgay, "Movement of Tagged Sea Scallops on Georges Bank," 43(4) *Marine Fisheries Review* 19-25 (April 1981).

53. The possibility does exist, however, for scallops to show a substantial overlap in the larval stage. During the first four to six weeks of their lives, larvae probably drift with the surface currents and may travel anywhere from 100 to 300 kilometers. Scallop Management Plan, *supra* note 51, at 11-12. Canadian scallop grounds, therefore, could depend on healthy scallop beds in U.S. waters, and vice versa. At present, the relationship between parent stock size and subsequent recruitment is not understood. *Id.* at 7.

54. Fisheries of the U.S., 1980, *supra* note 22, at 3.

55. Canadian Annual Statistical Review, *supra* note 23, at 47.

56. Scallop Management Plan, *supra* note 51, at 35 (Table 311).

57. *Id.*

58. *Id.* at 6.

59. *Id.* at 35 (table 311).

60. Canadian scallops make up 70 percent of U.S. scallop imports and from 1955 to 1980 accounted for 40 percent of U.S. consumption. *Id.* at 48.

61. Such a conflict might be fanned by the unsettled nature of international law as to access rights for foreign fleets to coastal state fishing zones. Articles 61 and 62 of the Law of the Sea Convention leave open to debate whether access rights are discretionary or mandatory upon the coastal state. *See* U.N. Doc. A/CONF. 62/L. 78 (August 28, 1981).

62. Draft Environmental Statement Appendices, *supra* note 15, at 111; S.H. Clark, Gulf of Maine, and Georges Bank Pollock Assessment Update," Northeast Fisheries Center, Lab. Ref. No. 79-59, 1 (December 1979) [hereinafter referred to as Pollock Assessment Update]. Some evidence also exists for limited spawning on the Scotian Shelf. *Id.* Draft Environmental Statement Appendices, *supra* note 15, at 111.

63. Hare, *supra* note 20, at 3.

64. Pollock Assessment Update, *supra* note 62, at 3.

65. Canadian Annual Statistical Review, 1979, *supra* note 23, at 47.

66. Pollock Assessment Update, *supra* note 62, at 3.

67. Fisheries of the U.S., 1980, *supra* 22, at 1.

68. Summary of Stock Assessments, *supra* note 25, at 11.

69. U.S. and Canadian landings have been essentially unregulated since 1977 when both countries withdrew from the International Commission for the Northeast Atlantic Fisheries (ICNAF), which had set quotas for pollock from 1973 to 1976. Pollock Assessment Update, *supra* note 62, at 2.

70. Fishery Management Plan for the Squid Fishery of the Northwest Atlantic Ocean, 44 Fed. Reg. 37257, 37260 (June 26, 1979). Three other species of Illex squid also inhabit the Atlantic ocean: *Illex coindetil* (in the eastern Atlantic, Mediterranean, Adriatic, Caribbean, Gulf of Mexico, and eastern coast of south Florida), *Illex argentinus* (along the coast of Argentina), and *Illex oxygonius* (from New Jersey to Florida and the Gulf of Mexico). C.F.E. Roper and C.C. Lu, "Rhynchoteuthion Larvae of Omastrephid Squids of the Western North Atlantic, with the First Description of Larvae and Juveniles of Illex illecebrosus," *Fisheries and Marine Serv. Tech. Rept. No. 833,* 14.1 (Proceedings of the Workshop on the Squid Illex illecebrosus, Dalhousie University, Halifax, Nova Scotia, May 1978) [hereinafter referred to as Proceedings on Squid].

71. Report of ICNAF Standing Committee on Research and Statistics, Special Meeting on Squid (February 1978), ICNAF Redbook, 1978, at 24. There is also an inshore movement along the New England-Middle Atlantic coastline. Fishery Management Plan for the Squid Fishery of the Northwest Atlantic Ocean, 44 Fed. Reg. 37257, 37260 (June 26, 1979) [hereinafter referred to as Squid Management Plan].

72. Initial larval studies may support such a theory. After hatching off the New England-Middle Atlantic region (and perhaps farther north and south, as well), squid larvae appear to travel seaward and to develop as juveniles offshore in slope waters and the Gulf Stream. Proceedings on Squid, *supra* note 70, at 14.11.

73. Dept. Fisheries and Oceans, Communications Branch, "Canada's Atlantic Squid Fishery," *Fishermen's Information Bulletin* 4 (1981).

74. U.S. officials have recognized the substantial overlap potential by referring to Illex as probable to "be transboundary in nature irrespective of

the final delimitation." *See* National Marine Fisheries Service, *A Short Run Economic Impact Analysis of the U.S.-Canadian Agreement on East Coast Fishery Resources* 2 (October 1979) [hereinafter referred to as Economic Impact Analysis].

75. For a history of commercial exploitation, *see* Squid Management Plan, *supra* note 71, at 37275.

76. Economic Impact Analysis, *supra* note 74, at 69 (Table 27).

77. U.S. statistics give only a combined figure for both Illex and Loligo squid. Thus the Illex figure had to be estimated by assuming nearly a fifty-fifty split in Illex and Loligo catches. Such an assumption seems justified since from 1975 to 1978, Illex catches averaged 916 tons per year compared to Loligo catches of 936 tons per year. *Id.* The 1979 combined squid catch was 6,696 tons valued at $4.27 million. Fisheries of the U.S., 1980, *supra* note 22, at 3.

Canadian statistics also give a combined figure for both Illex and Loligo. Canadian Annual Statistical Review, 1979, *supra* note 23, at 47. However, the catch may be assumed to consist almost entirely of Illex, since statistics from 1975 to 1978 show Canada's take of Loligo to be an almost negligible 4.4 tons per year. Economic Impact Analysis, *supra* note 74, at 69 (Table 27).

78. Draft Environmental Statement Appendices, *supra* note 15, at 107.

79. For a good summary of U.S. tagging studies, *see* J.S. Krouse, "Summary of Lobster, Homarus americanus, Tagging Studies in American Waters (1898-1978)," *Can. Tech. Rep. Fish. Aquat. Sci. No. 932*, pp. 135-140 (Proceedings of the Canada-U.S. Workshop on Status of Assessment Science for the N.W. Atlantic Lobster (Homarus americanus) Stocks, March 1980) [hereinafter referred to as American Tagging Studies]. For a good summary of Canadian tagging studies, see A.B. Stasko, "Tagging and Lobster Movements in Canada," *Can. Tech. Rep. Fish Aq. Sciences No. 932,* pp. 141-150 (Proceedings of the Canada-U.S. Workshop on Status of Assessment Science for the N.W. Atlantic Lobster (Homarus americanus) Stocks, March, 1980) [hereinafter referred to as Lobster Movements in Canada].

80. Gusey, *supra* note 10, at 487. The greatest reported migration is 426 kilometers (230 nautical miles) in fourteen months. Lobster Movements in Canada, *supra* note 79, at 143. At least one lobster has crossed from Browns Bank to Georges Bank. *Id.* at 147.

81. American Tagging Studies, *supra* note 79, at 139.

82. Only scallops ranked higher in the United States in 1979 and 1980. Fisheries of the U.S., 1980, *supra* note 22, at 1-3. Scallops, having a landed value of $66.80 million in 1980, ranked higher than lobster to fishermen of Nova Scotia, New Brunswick and Prince Edward Island. Maritime Annual Report, 1980, *supra* note 24, at 1.

83. Fisheries of the U.S., 1980, *supra* note 22, at 3.

84. Canadian Annual Statistical Review, 1979, *supra* note 23, at 47.

85. Economic Impact Analysis, *supra* note 74, at 69 (table 27).

86. *Id.*

87. Hare, *supra* note 20, at 5.

88. Draft Environmental Statement Appendices, *supra* note 15, at 89.

89. Hare, *supra* note 20, at 5 (Figure 10).

90. *Id.* at 5. The possibility exists that argentine consists of a single stock complex. *See* R.G. Halliday, *A Review of the Atlantic Argentine with Particular Reference to the Scotian Shelf*, ICNAF Research Doc. 74/21 (1974).

91. The USSR initiated the fishery in 1963 and was joined by Japan in 1971. Draft Environmental Statement Appendices, *supra* note 15, at 89.

92. Summary of Stock Assessments, *supra* note 25, at 20-21.

93. *See* Canadian Annual Statistical Review, 1979, *supra* note 23. Recent projections, however, have included a domestic catch of 1,102 tons in 1980. Dept. Fisheries and Oceans, *Resource Prospects For Canada's Atlantic Fisheries 1981-1987* 47 (February, 1981) [hereinafter referred to as Resource Prospects 1981-1987]. In 1978 only Nova Scotia entered into a cooperative arrangement for the meager amount of 47 tons valued at $6,000. In 1979 there were no cooperative arrangements. Canadian Annual Statistical Review, 1979, *supra* note 23, at 48-49.

94. Gusey, *supra* note 10, at 371. Draft Environmental Statement Appendices, *supra* note 15, at 93.

95. Gusey, *supra,* note 10, at 373 (figure 4.43).

96. *Id.* at 371.

97. Fisheries of the U.S., 1980, *supra* note 22, at 1.

98. Canadian Annual Statistical Review, 1979, *supra*, note 23, at 47. At least seventeen species rank higher in commercial value than cusk in 1979. *Id.*

99. For a general discussion of redfish distribution, *see* W. Templeman, "Redfish Distribution in the North Atlantic," *in ICNAF Spec. Publ. No. 3* 154-156 (ICES/ICNAF Redfish Symposium, 1961).

100. Hare, *supra* note 20, at 2. Other major concentrations occur on the Laurentian Channel edge and off southern Nova Scotia. *Id.*

101. *Id.*

102. For a discussion of redfish exploitation history in the northwest Atlantic, *see* R.K. Mayo et al., "An Assessment of the Gulf of Maine Redfish, Sebastes marinus (L.), Stock in 1978," Northeast Fisheries Center, Lab. Ref. No. 79-20, pp. 4-5 (May 1979).

103. Fisheries of the U.S., 1980, *supra* note 22, at 1.

104. Canadian Annual Statistical Review, 1979, *supra* note 23, at 47.

105. Economic Impact Analysis, *supra* note 74, at 69 (table 27).

106. U.S. Dept of Commerce, *Preliminary Management Plan for Hake Fisheries of the Northwest Atlantic,* 42 Fed. Reg. 10146, 10147 (February 18, 1977) [hereinafter referred to as Hake Preliminary Plan] .

107. Hare, *supra* note 20, at 3.

108. Such distinctions are based partly on scientific information but also on ICNAF management tradition. E.D. Anderson, F.E. Lax, and F.P. Almzida, "The Silver Hake Stocks and Fishery Off Northeastern United States" Northeast Fisheries Center, Lab. Ref. No. 79-28, p. 5 (July 10, 1979).

109. *Id.*

110. *Id.* at 3.

111. Fisheries of the U.S., 1980, *supra* note 22, at 1.

112. Canadian Annual Statistical Review, 1979, *supra* note 23, at 47. The combined catch for 1979 was 12,984 tons valued at $2.67 million.

113. Draft Environmental Statement Appendices, *supra* note 15, at 99.

114. U.S. Dept. of State, *United States-Canada East Coast Fishery Resources Agreement Data Summary* table I-13 (Washington, D.C., 1978) [hereinafter referred to as East Coast Agreement Data Summary].

115. Resource Prospects 1981-1987, *supra* note 93, at 46.

116. *Id.*

117. Draft Environmental Statement Appendices, *supra* note 15, at 99. U.S. catches from Georges Bank averaged about 18,200 tons per year. Catches from the Gulf of Maine averaged 29,700 tons per year. Anderson et al., *supra* note 108, at 8, 9-10.

118. East Coast Agreement Data Summary, *supra* note 114, at table I-13.

119. *Id.*

120. *Id.*

121. Draft Environmental Statement Appendices, *supra* note 15, at 97.

122. Hare, *supra* note 20, at 4. This assumption appears to be primarily based on ICNAF management divisions rather than scientific information. One researcher has postulated two discrete stocks, the first inhabiting southern Georges Bank and the second extending southward to Cape Cod. Another has indicated the possibility of three stocks: one Gulf of Maine-northern Georges stock and two southern stocks. Hake Preliminary Plan, *supra* note 106, at 10147.

123. Hare, *supra* note 20, at 4.

124. Gusey, *supra* note 10, at 399. *Also see* A.H. Leim and W.B. Scott, *Fishes of the Atlantic Coast of Canada* 218 (1966).

125. Gusey, *supra* note 10, at 402.

126. Fisheries of the U.S., 1980, *supra* note 22, at 1.

127. Canadian statistics generally give a combined hake catch. *See* Canadian Annual Statistical Review, *supra* note 23, at 47.

128. East Coast Agreement Data Summary, *supra* note 114, at table I-14. Red hake landings from the Gulf of Maine have not been of sufficient magnitude to justify separate assessment consideration. Hake Preliminary Plan, *supra* note 106, at 10148.

129. *Id.*

130. Resource Prospects 1981-1987, *supra* note 93, at 58.

131. Hare, *supra* note 20, at 4.

132. Gusey, *supra* note 10, at 399.

133. Hare, *supra* note 20, at 5.

134. Gusey, *supra* note 10, at 399. *Also see* Leim and Scott, *supra* note 124, at 218.

135. Economic Impact Analysis, *supra* note 74, at 69 (Table 27). U.S. catches from 1951 to 1974 averaged 3,530 tons per year. Gusey, *supra* note 10, at 404.

136. U.S. Dept. of Commerce, *Fisheries of the U.S., 1979* 1 (1979); Fisheries of the U.S., 1980, *supra* note 22, at 1.

137. Summary of Stock Assessments, *supra* note 25, at 20.

138. Mid-Atlantic Fishery Management Council, *Final Environmental Impact Statement/Fishery Management Plan for the Squid Fishery of the Northwest Atlantic Ocean* 8 (April 1978). Four additional Loligo species also frequent the Atlantic Ocean. *Id.* 72.

139. Draft Environmental Statement Appendices, *supra* note 15, at 118.

140. For a brief overview of the Loligo stock status, *see* A. Lange, "Squid (Loligo pealei and Illex illecebrosus) Stock Status Update: July, 1979," Northeast Fisheries Center, Lab. Ref. No. 79-30 (July 23, 1979).

141. Canadian harvests averaged less than 5 tons a year from 1975 to 1978. Economic Impact Analysis, *supra* note 74, at 69 (table 27).

142. *Id.*

143. Hare, *supra* note 20, at 6.

144. O.E. Sette, "Biology of the Atlantic Mackerel of North America Part II: Migrations and Habits," 51 U.S. *Fish & Wildlife Serv. Bull.* 251-315 (1950).

145. Hare, *supra* note 20, at 6.

146. D.W. Kulka and W.T. Stobo, "Winter Distribution and Feeding of Mackerel on the Scotian Shelf and Outer Georges Bank with Reference to the Winter Distribution of Other Finfish Species," *Can. Tech. Rep. Fish. Aquat. Sci. No. 1038* 1 (August 1981).

147. Draft Environmental Statement Appendices, *supra* note 15, at 109.

148. Fishery Management Plan for the Atlantic Mackerel Fishery of the Northwest Atlantic Ocean, 44 Fed. Reg. 53199 (Sept. 13, 1979) [hereinafter referred to as Mackerel Plan].

149. U.S. catch statistics for mackerel are available back to 1804. Canadian landing data is available back to 1876. For a listing of the historical catches, *see id.* at 53227 (Table 20).

150. *Id.*

151. Figures include catches from Nova Scotia, New Brunswick, and Prince Edward Island. Maritimes Annual Report, 1980, *supra* note 24, at 1.

152. Fisheries of the United States, 1980, *supra* note 22, at 1.

153. E.D. Anderson and W.J. Overholtz, "Status of the Northwest Atlantic Mackerel Stock—1979," Northeast Fisheries Center, Lab. Ref. No. 79-35 (August 1979).

154. Mackerel Plan, *supra* note 148, at 53197; Fisheries of the United States, 1980, *supra* 22, at 1.

155. Greg Peacock, senior adviser on pelagics, Dept. Fisheries and Oceans, Scotia-Fundy Region (personal interview, June 22, 1982).

156. Personal communication, Department of Fisheries and Oceans official.

The U.S. Fisheries-Management System

State Regulation of Marine Fisheries

State regulation of the offshore fisheries can be summarized under four categories: state control before March 1, 1977,[1] within the three-mile territorial sea; state control before March 1, 1977, beyond the three-mile territorial sea; state control after March 1, 1977, within the territorial sea; and state control after March 1, 1977, beyond the territorial sea.[2]

State Control Pre-1977 within the Territorial Sea

The first U.S. Supreme Court case to consider state control over marine fisheries crowned states with absolute ownership of the resource. In *McCready* v. *Virginia*,[3] the Court, upholding Virginia's right to limit oyster planting in state tidal waters to residents alone, stated:

> These [fisheries] remain under the exclusive control of the State, which has consequently the right . . . to appropriate its tide-waters and their beds to be used by its people as a common for taking and culti-vating fish. . . . Such an appropriation is in effect nothing more than a regulation of the use by the people of their common property. . . . It is in fact, a property right, and not a mere privilege or immunity of citizenship.[4]

Subsequent cases, however, gradually chipped away at the exclusive state control of marine fisheries. In *Manchester* v. *Massachusetts*, the Court upheld Massachusetts' right to regulate the offshore menhaden fishery but reserved the question whether Congress could override state regulation.[5] In *Louisiana* v. *Mississippi*, the Court changed its terminology to something less than full ownership: "The maritime belt is that part of the sea which, in contradistinction to the open sea, is *under the sway* of the riparian states."[6] In *Missouri* v. *Holland*, the Court limited the state ownership doctrine to wildlife actually captured.[7] Finally, in *Toomer* v. *Witsell* the Supreme Court labeled the concept of ownership as nothing but a legal fiction that expressed the state's "power to preserve and regulate the exploitation of an important resource." Paramount power over the fisheries in the territorial sea would rest with the federal government.[8]

Federal reign over the territorial sea was short-lived, however, for in 1953

Congress passed the Submerged Lands Act, which granted the states ownership and development rights in the seabed and natural resources of the territorial sea.[9] Except for federal reservations of "commerce, navigation, national defense, and international affairs" powers, states would enjoy full power to regulate the fisheries in the territorial sea according to state laws.[10]

State Control Pre-1977 beyond the Territorial Sea

States reached their regulatory hands to grasp control of marine fisheries beyond the three-mile territorial sea in three ways: landing laws, citizen control, and noncitizen control.

Landing Laws: A landing law is a state statute that authorizes state regulation of fish caught beyond the territorial sea and subsequently transported into the territorial sea.[11] Such laws were upheld by the U.S. Supreme Court on two grounds.[12] First, landing laws were essential for law enforcement. If states could not regulate beyond the territorial sea, fishermen could catch fish within state waters and simply move beyond state waters to avoid enforcement. Second, landing laws were necessary to promote conservation of local migratory fish. If states could not regulate beyond the territorial sea, fishermen could overfish local stocks whenever the fish ventured into the high seas.

Citizen Control: States also asserted the right to regulate the fishing of their own citizens upon the high seas. Unlike landing-law jurisdiction, fishermen would not have to transport their catches into state waters for enforcement to be valid. State officials could apprehend state citizens on the high seas.

Such jurisdiction was upheld by the U.S. Supreme Court in *Skiriotes* v. *Florida.*[13] There a Florida statute prohibited the use of diving gear to harvest sponges. A Florida citizen, diving for sponges with deep-sea gear, was apprehended beyond Florida's territorial sea and subsequently convicted.[14] The Supreme Court affirmed the conviction on the basis of citizen control:

> If the United States may control the conduct of its citizens upon the high seas, we see no reason why the State of Florida may not likewise govern the conduct of its citizens upon the high seas with respect to matters in which the State has a legitimate interest and where there is no conflict with Acts of Congress.[15]

Noncitizen Control: Under this approach, a state would claim the right to regulate and arrest noncitizens on the high seas in order to conserve a fish resource that migrates back and forth between the territorial sea and high seas.

Such an approach was upheld by the Alaska Supreme Court in *State* v. *Bundrant*.[16] There the Alaska Board of Fish and Game, wanting to conserve king crabs, closed the king crab season within the territorial sea and in a biological-influence zone extending into the Bering Sea. Washington residents, who ignored the closure, were subsequently arrested on the high seas and convicted. The Alaska Supreme Court, rejecting constitutional arguments against state power, affirmed the convictions based upon the need to prevent harm within the state.[17]

In the early 1970s, four of the five New England coastal states made extensive statutory claims to fisheries regulation beyond the territorial sea. Maine declared ownership and control over the harvesting of living resources out to 200 miles or the edge of the continental shelf, whichever was greater.[18] New Hampshire made a similar claim but disclaimed any enforcement powers until the governor made a proclamation of public necessity.[19] Rhode Island and Massachusetts claimed regulatory control of fishing within 200 miles or out to 100 fathoms, whichever was greater.[20] Only Connecticut failed to make a regulatory claim beyond the territorial sea.[21]

The legitimacy of such statutes was highly suspect on two grounds. First, Congress, in 1966, had indicated an intent to limit state control over fisheries to the territorial sea.[22] Second, the language of two 1950 Supreme Court cases indicated the federal government had exclusive control over natural resources beyond the territorial sea.[23]

On the other hand, arguments could be made for state extraterritorial ownership or control of marine fisheries. First, Congress had previously shown a clear intent to control only the seabed, not the fisheries or water above the seabed.[24] Second, in the 1950 cases the Supreme Court was called upon only to decide ownership of the seabed and subsoil, not ownership or control of the marine resources above the ocean floor. Thus, any language indicating federal ownership rights in the high seas fishery resources was just dictum.[25]

State Control Post-1977 within the Territorial Sea

In the Magnuson Fishery Conservation and Management Act (MFCMA), whereby Congress claimed federal control of a 197-mile fisheries zone contiguous to the territorial sea, Congress expressly reserved state rights to control the fish stocks within the territorial sea.[26] States retain the same control as before March 1, 1977, unless the secretary of commerce preempts state control through a four-step process:

1. Hold a public adjudicatory hearing.
2. Find a federal fisheries-management plan covering the state fishery.

3. Find the fishery predominantly occurring within the fisheries-conservation zone and beyond such zone.

4. Find state action or inaction to be in substantial and adverse conflict with the carrying out of the federal plan.[27]

Since the secretary of commerce has exercised such power only once to date, states continue to exert almost total management control over the near-shore fisheries.[28] The broad extent of such control is demonstrated by a few statistics. Ninety-nine percent of Atlantic menhaden is taken from the territorial sea, as well as the majority of striped bass, lobsters, crabs, and shellfish.[29] In 1980, over four times more Atlantic herring and nearly three times more Atlantic squid were harvested from the territorial sea than from the 3- to 200-mile zone.[30] Overall, twice as much fish was landed from state waters than from federal waters.[31]

State Control Post-1977 beyond the Territorial Sea

At first glance, Congress has severely restricted state control beyond the territorial sea. The MFCMA provides, "No State may directly or indirectly regulate any fishing . . . by any fishing vessel outside its boundaries, unless such vessel is registered under the laws of such state."[32] Such language would appear to close the doors of landing laws, citizen control, and noncitizen control and to leave states with the narrow regulatory door of vessel registration. However, since the MFCMA does not define vessel registration and since Congress added the phrase only at the last moment in conference committee and failed to comment on the phrase's meaning, states may interpret the vessel-registration door to be as wide or wider than the pre-MFCMA bases of jurisdiction.[33] The laws of three states show just such a movement.

In 1977 Oregon reclaimed landing-law jurisdiction by an innovative statutory definition of vessel registration. The statute states:

> The licensing of any boat pursuant to this chapter to take food fish for commercial purposes from the waters of this state or *land food fish from the waters of the Pacific Ocean* at any point in this state shall constitute *registration of such vessel* under the laws of this state for the purposes of the Fishery Conservation and Management Act of 1976.[34]

California has reclaimed citizen control jurisdiction by judicial decision in *California* v. *Weeren.*[35] There two California citizens were apprehended beyond the territorial seas for catching swordfish with the aid of a spotter plane in contravention of California law. Since the defendants' nineteen-ton vessel was registered under both federal and state laws, the defendants argued that California could not exercise jurisdiction over a federally registered vessel in the fisheries-conservation zone.[36] The California Supreme Court rejected the argument and interpreted the MFCMA to at least grant citizen control power to the States:

> We conclude that Section 1856 (a), fairly read, is intended to permit a state to regulate . . . the fishing of its citizens on adjacent waters, when not in conflict with federal law, when there exists a legitimate . . . state interest served by the regulation, and when the fishing is from vessels which are registered by it and operated from ports under its authority.[37]

Maine has perhaps reclaimed noncitizen control by defining registered vessel to include any vessel bringing a marine organism into the state's 200-mile offshore jurisdiction.[38] Only future judicial decisions or congressional legislative amendment will determine whether such a claim is valid.

Federal Regulation of Marine Fisheries

Before 1976 federal involvement in marine-fisheries management might be described as legal motions without much practical clout. In 1945 President Harry Truman notified the world of U.S. intent to establish high-seas fishery-conservation zones.[39] In 1949 the United States invited nine other countries to Washington, D.C., to join in a management scheme for the North Atlantic.[40] Not until 1966 did the United States actively legislate to protect the fisheries, and then the United States claimed only a nine-mile fisheries-conservation zone.[41]

In 1976 many political forces were opposed to any further protection of the fisheries by unilateral action. The president and State Department, worried about antagonizing other countries into a fish war, desired to extend U.S. fisheries jurisdiction by peaceful negotiation at the United Nations Conference on the Law of the Sea (UNCLOS III).[42] The Defense Department feared that any unilateral extension of fisheries jurisdiction by the United States would coax other countries to declare exaggerated jurisdictional claims which could interfere with the free passage of U.S. warships and submarines.[43] Tuna and shrimp fishermen, worried about foreign retaliations and closures of traditional fishing grounds, strongly lobbied against any bold U.S. action.[44]

Four major forces finally pushed Congress to extend unilaterally U.S. control over fisheries out to 200 miles. First, foreign fleets were fishing the Atlantic waters to the point of exhaustion. The American catch off New England fell from 100 percent in 1960 to a dismal 11.8 percent by 1975.[45]

Sixteen stocks were seriously depleted.[46] Foreign nations, left to self-enforcement, were not obeying international quotas. In 1975 alone, Russia overfished its mackerel quota by 100,000 metric tons and blamed the 100 percent overrun on "computer error."[47] Second, foreign fleets were mauling domestic fishing gear. Rhode Island fishermen alone needed $250,000 in federal assistance for damaged lobster pots and nets.[48] Third, the law-of-the-sea talks promised no early resolution, and even if there was early resolution, ratification might take over eight years.[49] Fourth, U.S. fishermen, seeing their livelihoods being vacuumed by foreign factory ships, united. Local cooperatives and associations grew in size and number. National organizations, such as the National Federation of Fishermen, assaulted Congress with a powerful lobby for unilateral action, action Congress finally took in passing the MFCMA.[50]

Because the MFCMA is the backbone of the U.S. fisheries-management system, a close examination of its vertebrae is essential to understanding the real flesh in operation. After proclaiming policy statements and definitions, the act speaks in four parts: the extent of U.S. authority, the extent of foreign fishing, the mechanics of the management system, and the effects of a law-of-the-sea treaty.[51]

Extent of U.S. Authority

The United States defines the scope of fisheries jurisdiction by making three claims and one disclaimer. The United States claims exclusive management authority over all fish within a 197-mile zone contiguous to the territorial sea; the right to manage anadromous species throughout their migratory range, except where they enter foreign waters; and the right to manage continental-shelf fishery resources beyond the fishery-conservation zone. It disclaims the right to manage highly migratory species of tuna within the conservation zone.[52]

Extent of Foreign Fishing

Before a foreign country may fish within the U.S. fishery-conservation zone, four conditions must be met. First, the country must negotiate with the secretary of state and enter into a governing international fisheries agreement (GIFA). In the agreement, the foreign country must agree to abide by all U.S. fisheries regulations, to allow vessel inspections at any time, to pay the costs of U.S. observers and to pay for all damage to U.S. fishing gear.[53] Second, a regional council must find a surplus of fish that foreigners will be allowed to catch.[54] Third, the secretary of state must allot a portion of the surplus to the particular country.[55] Such allocation must be based on the country's historic fishing rights, cooperation with the United States in fisheries research and enforcement, and cooperation in the International Whaling Convention.[56] Fourth, Congress must not veto the agreement.[57]

Recent amendment to the MFCMA will muzzle foreign fishing rights even further.[58] A mandatory phase-out formula will automatically reduce each country's catch from 5 to 15 percent per year and could eliminate all foreign fishing in U.S. waters by 1990.[59] Observer coverage of foreign fishing vessels will be increased to 100 percent, and a foreign country's fish allocation will depend on favorable tariffs towards U.S. fish exports.[60]

The MFCMA also bids other countries to bestow liberal fishing rights upon U.S. fishermen. If a country fails to give reciprocal fishing rights to U.S. fishermen or if a country seizes U.S. fishing vessels in disputed waters, the secretary of treasury may ban importation of that country's fish products.[61]

Mechanics of the Management System

The third section of the MFCMA establishes the particulars of the federal fisheries-management process.

The federal structure of fisheries management might be described as regional workhorses guided by federal reins or as a unique mix of regionalization and federalization. Most of the management work is delegated to eight regional councils, each responsible for formulating a management plan for each offshore fishery.[62] Assisting each council is a scientific and statistical committee, which generally advises on scientific issues and may gather and interpret scientific data, and advisory panels that provide practical guidance for each management plan.[63] The number of council members varies from a low of seven voting members in the Caribbean Council to a high of nineteen members in the Mid-Atlantic Council.

The New England Council, which has the greatest potential to affect U.S.-Canadian fisheries relations on the East Coast, has seventeen voting members and four nonvoting members. The voting members are five heads of state marine fisheries departments, one regional director of the National Marine Fisheries Service, and eleven at-large members appointed by the secretary of commerce from nominees submitted by state governors. The four nonvoting members are the regional director of the Fish and Wildlife Service (Department of Interior), the district commander of the Coast Guard, the executive director of the Atlantic States Marine Fisheries Commission, and a State Department representative.[64]

Responsible for actual development and oversight of New England Council plans are five committees: the large-pelagics committee (covering sharks, swordfish, and billfish), the herring committee, the lobster committee, the scallop committee, and the demersal finfish committee. Each oversight committee is composed of five council members plus from seven to twenty advisers drawn from an advisory panel of approximately ninety members.[65]

At the federal level, the secretary of commerce issues the actual fishing regulations to implement the management plans and makes certain the councils obey legislative guidelines. The secretary operates primarily through an agency of the Department of Commerce, the National Oceanic and Atmospheric Administration (NOAA), which in turn delegates much of the fishery work to the National Marine Fisheries Service (NMFS).[66] (See figure 2-1.)

The MFCMA establishes a five-step process of plan implementation:

Actual Formulation: Actual formulation of management plans involves three processes: scientific research must be undertaken and scientific data gathered; a management plan must be drafted; and, the plan must undergo federal review and public hearings.[67]

Regional councils are under no time pressure to formulate plans unless a specific fishery requires conservation and management. In such a case, a council would have to formulate a plan within a "reasonable time," a phrase left undefined. Otherwise the secretary of commerce could take control and independently implement a fisheries-management plan.[68]

Review by Secretary of Commerce: After a regional council completes the drafting and public hearings for a fisheries-management plan, the plan is submitted to the secretary of commerce for review. The secretary has up to sixty days to check with the secretary of state (to ascertain the foreign relations implications), to confer with the Coast Guard (to weigh enforcement implications), and to make sure the plan meshes with other applicable laws and seven national standards. If the secretary disapproves a plan, the plan is returned to the regional council, which then has forty-five additional days to correct or amend it. If the secretary still disapproves after council changes, the secretary may draft his or her own plan, which must be submitted to the regional council for comment. Thereafter the secretary may disregard or follow council suggestions and implement the plan.[69]

Publication in *Federal Register:* Each management plan is published in the *Federal Register*. Then the public has forty-five days in which to send written comments to the secretary of commerce.[70]

Public Hearing: The secretary of commerce is given discretion to hold a public hearing on the plan as a last-minute check on public opinion.[71]

Promulgation of Regulations: As the final step the secretary of commerce publishes the actual fishing regulations in the *Federal Register,* so the public will be put on notice.[72]

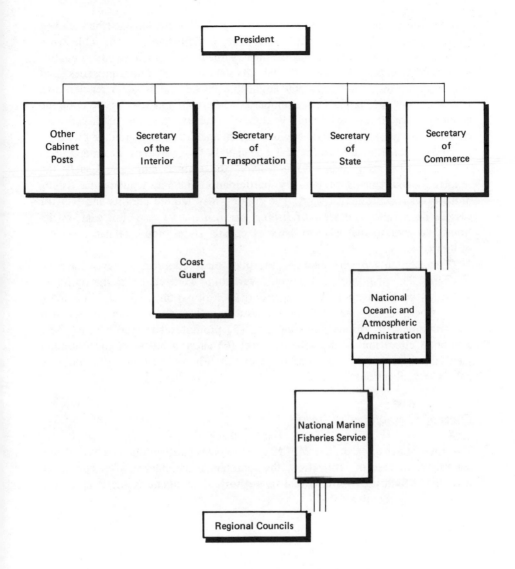

Figure 2-1. Administrative Overview of U.S. Fisheries Management

At the core of the fisheries-management plan is a summary of who gets what amount of fish. The council must determine the overall optimum yield of the fishery, the amount of the yield U.S. fishermen will harvest, the amount of the yield foreign fishermen may harvest, and the processing capacity of U.S. fish processors.[73]

An enormous amount of supportive data for the figures must be included in the plan. The council must state the overall management objectives, describe the stock(s) comprising the management unit (such as any predator-prey relationships), describe fish habitats (spawning grounds, nurseries, and migratory routes), summarize any applicable laws (treaties, state regulations), review current fishing practices (number of fishermen and vessels), describe the economic conditions of fishing (value of catches, incomes of fishermen), describe the markets for fish, explore the sociocultural backgrounds of fishermen (ages, educational backgrounds), and specify the sources of the data.[74]

To assist conservation of the fishery, the council must also specify the reporting requirements of industry participants and may regulate the fishing industry in six alternative ways. The council may require permits and fees for vessels, limit times and areas of fishing, set fish quotas, establish gear restrictions, incorporate management laws of coastal states, and establish a system of limited entry.[75]

The contents of the management plan must conform to seven national standards. The plan must: (1) prevent overfishing while achieving the optimum yield; (2) be based upon the best scientific information available; (3) manage a fish stock, to the extent practicable, as a unit throughout its range; (4) treat the fishermen of various states equally; (5) promote efficiency but not have economic allocation as the sole purpose; (6) allow a buffer in the optimum yield figure to account for variations in the fish resource; and (7) minimize costs and duplications.[76]

Effect of a Law-of-the-Sea Treaty

The final subchapter of the MFCMA anticipates ratification of a law-of-the-sea treaty. In case of ratification, the secretary of commerce, after consulting with the secretary of state, would be authorized to amend regulations to conform to treaty requirements.[77]

Problems of the System

Since passage of the MFCMA, six major problems have plagued the U.S. fisheries-management system: the council role, council composition, scientific knowledge, plan implementation, enforcement, and poor attitudes of fishermen.[78]

Council Role

Are regional councils federal or regional entities? Are the councils dependent or independent? Are council members and staff federal employees or private employees? Such questions have bothered U.S. fisheries managers from the beginning and remain somewhat unresolved.

Strong arguments can be made for the nonfederal, independent status of the councils. The MFCMA itself grants councils almost exclusive plan-making powers and limits the federal role to reviewing plans for conformity with seven national standards and other laws.[79] The legislative history also supports the nonfederal character of the councils. The original House and Senate bills, which would have made the councils more federal in character, were rejected.[80] Language from the Joint Explanatory Statement of the Committee of Conference indicated the eleven at-large members of regional councils were not to be considered government employees.[81] Finally, congressmen, in various oversight hearings, have strongly emphasized the independent character of the councils.[82]

In fact, the councils have tended to be treated as federal advisory pawns. On occasion the National Marine Fisheries Service has issued fishing regulations without consulting the councils.[83] And sometimes the councils have acquiesced in federal drafting of management plans.[84] Councils have often been pressured to follow federal planning ideas through subtle federal warnings such as, "[D]o not submit that plan, because the Secretary is going to reject it."[85] Legal opinions from various federal agencies, such as the NOAA, the Department of Justice, and the General Services Administration, have labeled the councils as federal instrumentalities.[86]

Application of federal laws has threatened to undermine council plan making in two major ways. First, the Federal Advisory Committee Act's burdensome notice requirements may prevent councils from acting when emergency amendments to management plans are needed and may thwart councils from changing management plans rejected by the secretary of commerce.[87] Second, application of federal criminal conflict-of-interest statutes to the councils could prevent industry representatives on the councils from voting on management plans because of financial interest in the result. Also, the industry representatives may not be able to consider confidential statistical data because of competitive implications.[88]

The federal dependency of the councils may be explained by four factors. First, councils were like new workers in an established federal bureaucracy. Council members had to rely on federal officials to learn all the basics, such as who makes decisions and what guidelines to follow. A dependency once established may be difficult to overcome. Second, since council members are not full-time employees, meeting on an average of two to three days a month, a natural tendency would be to rely on full-time experts such as NMFS employees who have more time to devote to fisheries management. Third, Washington bureaucrats prefer established organizational lines and the advisory capacity is the line they are used to. Fourth, councils have relied on the Department of Commerce for funding and some staffing.[89]

Council Composition

Council memberships have tended to be dominated by representatives from the commercial and recreational fishing industries, as shown by 1979 statistics. Seventy-eight percent of the councils' at-large members were industry representatives, and industry representatives controlled a majority in the New England Council (ten out of eleven voting seats), the Gulf of Mexico Council (ten out of seventeen voting seats), the Caribbean Council (four out of seven voting seats), and the Pacific Council (seven out of thirteen voting seats). Other councils displayed a large share of industry representation. Industry representatives filled nine out of nineteen voting seats on the Mid-Atlantic Council, six out of thirteen voting seats on the South Atlantic Council, four out of eleven voting seats in the Western Pacific Council and three out of eleven voting seats in the North Pacific Council.[90]

Since the regulated tend to do the regulating, councils have arguably favored the subjective whims of the fishing industry rather than the objective needs of conservation and management. The New England Council provides two good examples. In 1978 the council's groundfish plan, based on biological data, recommended a catch of 6,000 metric tons of haddock, 27,500 metric tons of cod, and 8,100 metric tons of yellowtail flounder. When industry complained of low quotas, the council listened. In three emergency amendments the quotas soared to 28,254 metric tons of haddock and 66,340 metric tons of cod.[91]

Recent council plans show a move toward free-enterprise management where government regulation is kept to a minimum. The council's interim groundfish plan merely limits fish size and mesh size and closes spawning areas. Its scallop plan only limits scallop size (three and a quarter inches) and number of meats per pound (forty the first year, thirty effective May 15, 1983). The herring plan, while currently setting overall quotas (30,000 metric tons for the Gulf of Maine and 15,000 metric tons for Georges Bank and southern New England) may soon move in the same direction.[92]

Such plans, however, may also be rationalized in a more-positive light. According to the council's executive director, the council has seriously struggled with the proper balance of priorities: protection of the resource versus social and economic welfare of the industry. Emergency amendments may be viewed as an objective commitment to treat the economic woes of troubled fishermen. The move toward free enterprise may also be viewed as an interim phase on the path to multispecies management. In fact, the council is now working on a multispecies management regime.

Scientific Knowledge

Although a mass of scientific data must be collected for each fisheries-management plan and accompanying environmental-impact statement, the U.S.

fisheries management still suffers from a lack of scientific information. Little information has been gathered about recreational fishing catches, primarily because most states have no salt-water sportfishing license as a vehicle of data collection. Ecological research, particularly comprehensive studies of predator-prey relationships, is still in the stage of infancy. Sociological and economic data have been so sparse that management plans often must rely on an estimate of the biological condition of the stock as the only valid criterion for stock management.[93]

Plan Implementation

Given the numerous regulations and guidelines that a management plan must follow, plan implementation has become an administrative nightmare. After four months to a year of plan formulation, another 250 to 270 days is generally required for federal and public review. A simple regulatory amendment may take at least 120 days. The secretary of commerce has been forced to make emergency fishing regulations the rule rather than the exception.[94]

As a result of the slow implementation process, only twelve management plans were in effect nationwide as of December 31, 1980. As of July 1982, the New England Council has issued only three management plans: the Atlantic groundfish plan, the Atlantic herring plan, and the sea scallop plan.[95]

The NMFS is considering a number of alternatives to streamline the management process. Possible options are: limitation of the number of fisheries managed; integration of management plans, environmental-impact statements, and regulatory analyses into a single document to reduce duplication and processing;[96] provision of improved guidelines; and implementation of a framework approach to management plans. The framework approach would design plans to cover several years and to include adjustment formulas, so the lengthy amendment process could be bypassed.[97]

Enforcement

Enforcement of the MFCMA has suffered from four maladies. First, state regulations or lack of regulations have provided a wide loophole for fishermen to avoid federal management plans.[98] For example, Maine has imposed no restrictions on cod, haddock, or yellowtail flounder that can be harvested from its territorial waters. Fishermen have been able to catch thousands of pounds of groundfish illegally within the federal fishery zone and avoid punishment by claiming that the harvest occurred in state territorial waters.[99] Second, low budgets have made enforcement personnel in short supply. In 1979 the NMFS had fewer than thirty agents from Maine to Virginia and only five agents in

Massachusetts to cover nearly forty ports and over one thousand vessels.[100] Third, regulations have tended to be so complex and changing that enforcement officers have had difficulty knowing which law to enforce. For example, the Coast Guard issued citations for violations of the surf clam plan only to find the fishing was actually legal under an amended plan.[101] Fourth, prosecution of violators has tended to be slow and lackadaisical, with many cases taking years to settle and often with very small penalties.[102]

Attitudes of Fishermen

Many government officials have pointed to what may be the most-serious ailment in the U.S. fisheries-management system: fishermen who buck against any regulation. The tendency continues, particularly among New England fishermen, to view the fisheries-conservation zone as a fence built to keep out foreigners, not to control domestic fishing and to view any government action as an assault on independent life-styles.[103]

The statement of a Maine fishermen before the U.S. Senate further captures the hard-nose sense of independence:

> Woods Hole is a waste of money. It hasn't done one thing for the fishermen. They are marine biologists, and they say, "We assume. We assume," this and that. Assumptions, that is what they are basing this quota on. It isn't right.
>
> We could go shrimping. One man in the State of Maine, Vinal Look, says we can't go. Do you call that right?
>
> These foreign fish are coming in. That stuff is dipped in chemicals. It is against the Pure Food Act in this country. No one is watching out for it. It is against the law to bring a fish in Massachusetts round, with the stomachs on them.
>
> I have been to Grand Manion, coming in there with fish stomachs in them 10 days. They fillet them and ship them to Boston, Mass. . . . That is stupid.[104]

Notes

1. On March 1, 1977, the Fishery Conservation and Management Act, 16 U.S.C.A. §§ 1801-1882 (Supp. 1980), became effective and established a 197-mile fisheries-conservation zone contiguous to the three-mile territorial sea. The act was subsequently renamed the Magnuson Fishery Conservation and Management Act.

2. For a summary of the state role in marine fisheries regulation, *see*

Schoenbaum and McDonald, *State Management of Marine Fisheries after the Fishery Conservation and Management Act of 1976 and Douglas v. Seacoast Products, Inc.,* 19 Wm. & Mary L. Rev. 17 (1977-78), and Comment, *The Fisheries Conservation and Management Act of 1976: State Regulation of Fishing Beyond the Territorial Sea,* 31 Me. L. Rev. 303 (1980).

3. 94 U.S. 391 (1876).

4. *Id.* at 395.

5. 139 U.S. 240, 266 (1890).

6. 202 U.S. 1, 52 (1905) (emphasis added).

7. 252 U.S. 416 (1920). Justice Holmes stated, "To put the claim of the State upon title is to lean upon a slender reed. Wild birds are not in the possession of anyone; and possession is the beginning of ownership." *Id.* at 434.

8. 334 U.S. 385, 402 (1948). This federal paramountcy over fisheries sprang from federal paramountcy over the seabed, first recognized in *United States* v. *California,* 332 U.S. 19 (1947). There the Supreme Court granted the federal government the paramount right to exploit the petroleum and mineral resources of the territorial seabed even though California had granted leases for offshore development since the early 1920s. The Court based federal paramountcy on three pillars. First, since federal statesmen made the international claim to a three-mile territorial sea after formation of the federal union, the states never held title to a three-mile belt (Secretary of State Jefferson, in a note to the British minister in 1793, advanced the first official American claim for a three-mile zone). *Id.* at 33. Second, federal control of the territorial sea was essential for national defense and security. *Id.* at 35. Third, federal control was necessary for foreign commerce and international relations. *Id.*

For a discussion of the political forces behind the federal challenge to state power, *see* A. Hollick, *U.S. Foreign Policy and the Law of the Sea* 103-111 (1981).

9. 43 U.S.C.A. §§ 1301-1315 (1974). Natural resources were defined as including "oil, gas and all other minerals, and fish, shrimp, oysters, clams, crabs, lobsters, sponges, kelp, and other marine animal and plant life." *Id.* at § 1301(e). The act set a maximum limit on the seaward boundaries of the states at three miles in the Atlantic and Pacific oceans and nine miles in the Gulf of Mexico. *Id.* at §§ 1301(b), 1312. In subsequent litigation, the Supreme Court granted Florida and Texas a nine-mile limit and set a three-mile limit for the remaining Gulf states. *United States* v. *Louisiana et al.,* 363 U.S. 1 (1960); *United States* v. *Florida et. al.,* 363 U.S. 121 (1960).

10. 43 U.S.C.A. § 1314 (1974).

11. Washington's statute is exemplary: "Every person . . . operating a fishing vessel . . . used in the commercial taking or catching of salmon in *offshore waters* and transporting . . . the same in and through the *waters of the state of Washington* and delivering the same in any place or port in . . . Washington shall . . . obtain a permit from the director of fisheries." Wash. Rev. Code Ann. § 75.18.080 (Supp. 1980) (emphasis added).

12. *Bayside Fish Co.* v. *Gentry*, 297 U.S. 422 (1936). The Supreme Court upheld California's regulation of the volume of sardines (caught both within and without state waters) that could be reduced to fish meal.

13. 313 U.S. 69 (1941).

14. Although the width of Florida's territorial sea was in controversy, the Supreme Court assumed the offense to have occurred on the high seas. *Id.* at 76.

15. *Also see People* v. *Foretich*, 14 Cal. App. 3d 6, 92 Cal. Rptr. 481 (1970).

16. 546 P.2d 530 (Alaska), *appeal dismissed sub. nom. Uri* v. *State*, 429 U.S. 806 (1976). *Also see F/V American Eagle* v. *State*, 620 P.2d 657 (1980).

17. State fisheries regulations are always subject to constitutional reins. The most prevalent constitutional challenges have been: Privileges and Immunities (*Toomer* v. *Witsell*, 334 U.S. 385 (1948). Privileges and Immunities clause barred South Carolina from enforcing a nonresident shrimp license fee of $2,500 when residents had to pay only $25); Equal Protection (*Tukahashi* v. *Fish and Game Commission*, 334 U.S. 410 (1948). California Statute forbidding Japanese aliens from attaining commercial fishing licenses was declared unconstitutional); Federal Preemption (*Douglas* v. *Seacoast Products, Inc.*, 431 U.S. 265 (1977). Federal licensing pursuant to congressional commerce power, preempted Virginia's state regulation since the state laws were discriminatory and in direct conflict with federal law); Dormant Commerce Power (*Foster Packing Co.* v. *Haydel*, 278 U.S. 1 (1928). Louisiana Statute requiring all landed shrimp to be processed in Louisiana held invalid. *Hughes* v. *Oklahoma*, 441 U.S. 322 (1979). Oklahoma Statute banning the interstate shipment of live minnows held invalid); and the Treaty Power (*Missouri* v. *Holland*, 252 U.S. 416 (1920). Migratory Bird Treaty overrode state bird regulations.)

18. Me. Rev. Stat. Ann. tit. 1, § 2(2-A) (1979) (originally enacted in 1973).

19. N.H. Rev. Stat. Ann. Ch. 1 § 14-16, 18 (Supp. 1979) (originally enacted in 1973).

20. R.I. Gen. Laws § 20-36-1 (Supp. 1972). Mass. Ann. Laws Ch. 130, § 17 (1965), *as amended* (Supp. 1971). The Rhode Island statute was repealed effective January 1, 1982, and was replaced by R.I. Gen. Laws §§ 20-3-1 to 20-3-6 (Supp. 1980). The new law provides for a marine fisheries council to have regulatory jurisdiction over all marine animal species within the jurisdictional territory of the state. R.I. Gen Laws § 20-3-2 (Supp. 1980). Since jurisdictional territory is not defined, the extent of the offshore claim will be unclear. Criminal jurisdiction would be limited to the territorial sea. R.I. Gen. Laws § 12-3-5 (Supp. 1980).

21. Connecticut, of course, faces Long Island Sound and would have no reason to claim high-seas fishery jurisdiction. Other states making statutory claims to fisheries jurisdiction beyond the three-mile territorial sea were Oregon

(a fifty-mile fisheries-conservation zone), Or. Rev. Stat. § 506. 750-755 (1974), and North Carolina (regulation out to 200 miles or 100 fathoms), N.C. Gen. Stat. § 113-134.1 (1978 Repl.). For a general discussion of state fisheries zones, *see* Note, *Territorial Jurisdiction—Massachusetts Judicial Extension Act—State Legislature Extends Jurisdiction of State Courts to 200 Miles at Sea,* 5 Vand. J. Transnat'l L. 490 (1972), and Comment, *Constitutionality of State Fishery Zones in the High Seas: The Oregon Fisheries Conservation Zone Act,* 55 Or. L. Rev. 141 (1976).

22. The Bartlett Act, which established a nine-mile fishery zone contiguous to the territorial sea, provided: "Nothing in this chapter shall be construed as extending the jurisdiction of the States to the natural resources beneath and in the waters within the fisheries zone established in this chapter." 16 U.S.C.A. § 1094 (1974) (Repealed in 1977).

23. In *United States* v. *Louisiana,* 339 U.S. 699 (1950), the U.S. Supreme Court struck down Louisiana's claim to the seabed out to twenty-seven miles. In entering the decree the Court said: "The United States is now . . . possessed of paramount rights in, and full dominion and power over, the lands, minerals and *other things* underlying the Gulf of Mexico . . . extending seaward twenty-seven marine miles . . . of the State of Lousiana." 340 U.S. 899 (1950) (emphasis added). In *United States* v. *Texas,* 339 U.S. 707 (1950), the Court, in striking down Texas's claim to the seabed out to the edge of the continental shelf, stated: "Today the controversy is over oil. Tomorrow it may be over some other substance. . . . If the property, *whatever it may be,* lies seaward of low water mark, its use, disposition, management and control involve national interests and national responsibilities. That is the source of the national right in it." *Id.* at 719 (emphasis added). *Also see United States* v. *Maine,* 420 U.S. 515 (1975).

24. In the Outer Continental Shelf Lands Act of 1953, Congress, claiming the seabed and subsoil of the outer continental shelf, stated: "This subchapter shall be construed in such manner that the character as high seas of the water above the Continental Shelf and the right to navigation and fishing thereon shall not be affected." 43 U.S.C.A. § 1332(b) (1964).

25. At least two cases have distinguished between federal ownership of the seabed and nonownership of the resources and water above the seabed. *See Employers Mutual Casualty Co.* v. *Samuels,* 407 S.W. 2d 839 (Tex. Civ. App. 1966) (death above continental shelf not covered by an insurance policy, limiting coverage to death within the United States, since the United States owns only the seabed and not the super-adjacent waters) and *Treasure Salvors* v. *Unidentified Wreck, Etc.,* 569 F.2d 330 (5th Cir. 1978) (shipwreck resting on the continental shelf not owned by the federal government since U.S. ownership was limited to the seabed and subsoil).

26. 16 U.S.C.A. §§ 1801-1882, 1856 (Supp. 1980) (hereinafter referred to as the FCMA).

27. *Id.* at § 1856(b).

28. In May 1982 the secretary of commerce preempted Oregon's attempt to open the salmon season earlier than provided by the federal plan Personal interview, Douglas Marshall, executive director, New England Fisheries Management Council (July 16, 1982).

State control, of course, would still be subject to constitutional limitations. Based on the Submerged Lands Act, states would still have an ownership interest in the living resources of the territorial sea. *See* text accompanying note 9, *supra*. However, the Supreme Court has rejected ownership terminology in favor of regulatory language: "Under modern analysis, the question is simply whether the state has exercised its police power in conformity with federal laws and the Constitution." *Douglas* v. *Seacoast Products Inc.*, 431 U.S. 265, 284-285 (1977).

29. Commercial Fisheries Authorization and Oversight, H.R. 4890: Hearings before the Subcommittees on Fisheries and Wildlife Conservation and the Environment and Oceanography of the House Comm. on Merchant Marine and Fisheries, 96th Cong., 318-319 (February 11, 1980) (statement of Irwin M. Alperin, executive director, Atlantic States Marine Fisheries Commission).

30. Atlantic herring catches were 150.36 million pounds from within the territorial sea and 33.63 million pounds from beyond the territorial sea. U.S. Dept. of Commerce, *Fisheries of the United States, 1980* 8 (April, 1981). Atlantic squid catches were 6.58 million pounds from within the territorial sea and 2.23 million pounds from beyond the territorial sea. *Id.* at 10.

31. Total landings were 4.20 billion pounds from within the territorial sea compared to 2.03 billion pounds beyond the territorial sea. *Id.*

32. 16 U.S.C.A. § 1856(a) (Supp. 1980).

33. Senate Comm. on Commerce and Nat'l Ocean Policy Study, 94th Cong., 2d sess., A Legislative History of the Fishery Conservation and Management Act of 1976, 91 (Comm. Print 1976) [hereinafter referred to as Legislative History]. For a discussion of the possible interpretation of the vessel-registration phrase, *see* Comment, *The Fishery Conservation and Management Act of 1976: State Regulation of Fishing Beyond the Territorial Sea,* 31 Me. L. Rev. 303, 325-327 (1980).

34. Or. Rev. Stat. § 508.265 (1977) (emphasis added).

35. 607 P.2d 1279 (1980).

36. Fishing vessels of five tons or more must obtain a federal license (46 U.S.C.A. § 263 (1958) and must register at a state home port (46 U.S.C.A. §§ 18, 1012 (1976). Thus, fishing vessels below five tons will have only state registration, and vessels above five tons will have dual registration.

37. 607 P.2d at 1287.

38. Registered vessel is defined as "a vessel which is owned or operated by a person licensed under this Part, a vessel which is used to bring a marine organism into the state or its coastal waters or a vessel which is licensed

under . . . 46 U.S. Code, chapter 2 and 12 and section 808 and has declared at Maine home port." Me. Rev. Stat. Ann. tit. 12, § 6001 (36) (Supp. 1978-79). Coastal waters is defined to include waters within state marine jurisdiction. *Id.* at § 6001(6). State marine jurisdiction is defined as ownership of living resources out to 200 miles or the continental shelf. *Id.* at tit. 1, § 2(2-A) (1979). Thus, Maine claims the right not only to regulate state-licensed vessels and federal-state registered vessels but any vessel bringing fish into offshore waters. If the word *bringing* is defined narrowly, Maine might be limited to an expanded version of landing laws, one extending out to 200 miles. If the word *bringing* is interpreted broadly, Maine might be able to exert noncitizen control: the right to regulate any fisherman affecting an overlapping fish stock where there is no conflicting federal management plan.

39. Presidential Proclamation No. 2668, "Policy of the United States with Respect to Coastal Fisheries in Certain Areas of the High Seas," 59 Stat. 885, 10 Fed. Reg. 12304 (September 28, 1945). Truman also gave notice of U.S. intent to control the subsoil and seabed of the continental shelf. Presidential Proclamation No. 2667, "Policy of the United States with Respect to the Natural Resources of the Subsoil and Seabed of the Continental Shelf," 59 Stat. 884, 10 Fed. Reg. 12303 (September 28, 1945). For a general discussion of the Truman proclamations, *see* L. Juda, *Ocean Space Rights: Developing U.S. Policy* 11-20 (1975).

40. The invitees were Canada, Denmark, France, Great Britain, Iceland, Newfoundland, Norway, Portugal, and Spain. The conference gave birth to the Northwest Atlantic Fisheries Convention, which established a management body (the International Commission on Northwest Atlantic Fisheries, ICNAF) to investigate and protect the Northwest Atlantic fisheries. A. Hollick, *U.S. Foreign Policy and the Law of the Sea* 66-67 (1981).

41. Bartlett Act, 16 U.S.C.A. § 1091-1094 (1974) (repealed 1977).

42. Legislative History, *supra* note 33, at 860 (statement of Mr. Whitehurst).

43. *Id.* at 951 (statement of Mr. Stratton).

44. *Id.* at 952-953 (statement of Mr. Bennett).

45. *Id.* at 260 (statement of Mr. Weicker).

46. *Id.* at 239 (statement of Mr. Gravel).

47. *Id.* at 478 (statement of Mr. Stevens).

48. *Id.* at 237 (statement of Mr. Pastore).

49. *Id.* at 249-250 (statement of Mr. Stevens).

50. For a general discussion of the various U.S. lobby organizations, *see* S. Greene, *Washington: A Study of the U.S. Fish Policy Process,* 17-24 (1978).

51. 16 U.S.C.A. §§ 1801-1802 (Supp. 1980): subchapter I, Fishery Management Authority of the United States, *id.* at §§ 1811-1813; subchapter II, Foreign Fishing and International Fishery Agreements, *id.* at §§ 1821-1827;

subchapter III, National Fishery Management Program, *id.* at § § 1851-1861; subchapter IV, Miscellaneous Provisions, *id.* at § § 1881-1882.

52. Section 1811 provides, "There is established a zone contiguous to the territorial sea of the United States to be known as the fishery conservation zone. The inner boundary of the fishery conservation zone is a line coterminous with the seaward boundary of each of the coastal states, and the outer boundary of such zone is . . . 200 nautical miles from the baseline from which the territorial sea is measured."

Based upon the section's failure to define the seaward boundaries of the states, at least one commenter has argued that an extension of the territorial sea to twelve miles by a law-of-the-sea convention could cloak states with fisheries jurisdiction out to twelve miles. *See* Snow, *Extended Fishery Jurisdiction in Canada and the United States,* 5 Ocean Development and Int'l Law, 291, 302 (1978).

However, legislative history and case law make such a proposition dubious. The legislative history of the MFCMA shows clearly that state primary jurisdiction was not to extend beyond three miles. *See* Legislative History, *supra* note 33, at 459-461 (statement of Mr. Stevens). The U.S. Supreme Court has consistently refused to grant states paramountcy over the seabed within or beyond the territorial sea, and the Court's language indicates the same would hold true for state fishing rights. *See* note 23, *supra.*

16 U.S.C.A. § 1812(1)-(3), 1813 (Supp. 1980). The United States excluded tuna management from the act so other countries might follow suit and not interfere with U.S. tuna fishermen. Legislative History, *supra* note 33, at 863 (statement of Mr. Anderson).

53. 16 U.S.C.A. § 1821(c), 1822 (Supp. 1980).

54. *Id.* at § 1821(d). The regional councils determine the optimum yield for each fishery and subtract the amount that U.S. fishermen will harvest. The remainder, if any, will be surplus available to foreign fleets.

55. *Id.* at § 1821(e).

56. If a country has violated the Whaling Convention, the secretary of state may reduce that country's catch allotment by 50 percent or more. *Id.* at § 1821(e)(2)(13).

57. If Congress does not veto the agreement within sixty days, the agreement goes into effect. For a general discussion of the congressional-review process, *see* Note, *Congressional Authorization and Oversight of International Fishery Agreements under the Fishery Conservation and Management Act of 1976,* 52 Wash. L. Rev. 495 (1977).

58. American Fisheries Promotion Act of 1980, Pub. L. 96-561, tit. 2, 94 Stat. 3296 (codified in scattered sections of 16 U.S.C.A.).

59. 16 U.S.C.A. § 1821(d) (Special Supp. 1980). The complex formula uses 1979 harvests as base figures for calculation. Since Canada had no 1979 catch from U.S. waters, such a formula would preclude future Canadian fishery

in U.S. waters unless fishing rights are granted by treaty or legislative amendment. Such a formula may also violate emerging international law as reflected by the Draft Convention on the Law of the Sea. Articles 61 and 62 of the convention may be interpreted to require coastal states to grant fishing rights to foreign states, particularly developing states. Draft Convention on the Law of the Sea, U.S. Doc. A/CONF. 62/L. 78 (Aug. 28, 1981). For congressional debate on the international law implication, *see* (1980) U.S. Code Cong. & Ad. News 6879-6886. For a more-detailed analysis of the American Fisheries Promotion Act, *see* Note, *Law of the Sea: Protection of United States Fishing Interests—American Fisheries Promotion Act of 1980,* 22 Harv. Int'l L.J. 485 (1981).

60. 16 U.S.C.A. § 1821(i), (e) (Special Supp. 1980). In 1979 only 23.2 percent of foreign vessels, fishing off New England, carried American observers. (1980) U.S. Code Cong. & Ad. News 6890. Bureaucrats have labeled the allocation the "fish and chips" policy. The secretary of state is to use allocations as a bargaining tool for reducing tariff restrictions abroad and increasing the markets for U.S. fish. U.S. Dept. of Commerce, *Fishery Conservation and Management Act Operations Handbook* 46 (October 1980).

61. 16 U.S.C.A. § 1825 (Supp. 1980).

62. *Id.* at 1852(h) (1). The eight regional councils are: the New England Council representing Maine, New Hampshire, Massachusetts, Rhode Island, and Connecticut; the Mid-Atlantic Council representing New York, New Jersey, Delaware, Pennsylvania, Maryland, and Virginia; the South Atlantic Council representing North Carolina, South Carolina, Georgia, and Florida; the Caribbean Council representing the Virgin Islands and Puerto Rico; the Gulf Council representing Florida, Alabama, Louisiana, Mississippi, and Texas; the Pacific Council representing California, Oregon, and Washington; the North Pacific Council representing Alaska, Washington, and Oregon; and the Western Pacific Council representing Hawaii, American Samoa, and Guam. *Id.* at § 1852.

63. *Id.* at § 1852(g).

64. *Id.* at § 1852(b) (c). Five of the eleven at-large seats are obligatory; that is, each constituent state has one obligatory seat. U.S. Dept. Commerce, *Fishery Conservation Management Operations Handbook II* (October 1980).

The Atlantic States Fisheries Commission is composed of three representatives from each of the following states: Maine, New Hampshire, Massachusetts, Rhode Island, Connecticut, New York, New Jersey, Delaware, Maryland, Virginia, North Carolina, South Carolina, Georgia, and Florida. It was created by interstate compact in 1942 to coordinate fisheries regulations among the states. The commission has been relatively ineffective, however, since its powers are limited to holding consultations and making recommendations. *See* H. Knight and T. Jackson, *Legal Impediments to the Use of Interstate Agreements in Co-Ordinated Fisheries Management Programs: States in the N.M.F.S. Southeast Region* (September 28, 1973). For the text of the interstate compact, *see* Me. Rev. Stat. Ann. tit. 12, § § 4601-4613 (1964).

65. Personal interview, Douglas Marshall, executive director, New England Fisheries Management Council (July 16, 1982). For a critique of actual council meetings, see M. Estellie Smith, The "Public Face" of the New England Regional Fishery Council: Year 1 (Technical Report 78-36, Woods Hole Oceanographic Institution, April 1978).

66. For a general discussion of the administrative structure, see U.S. Dept. of Commerce, U.S. Ocean Policy in the 1970s: Status and Issues, III-11 to III-18 (1978).

67. A heavy layer of federal guidelines has made the actual formulation stage time-consuming and complex. For example, a draft management plan's environmental-impact statement must pass through five agency hands (the regional director of NMFS, the NMFS Office of Resource Conservation and Management, the Department of Commerce deputy assistant secretary for environmental affairs, the Department of Commerce Environmental Work Group, and the Environmental Protection Agency) just in the plan-development stage. Rogalski, The Unique Federalism of the Regional Councils under the Fishery Conservation and Management Act of 1976, 9 B.C. Env. Aff. L. Rev. 163, 182-183 (1980).

In 50 C.F.R. § 601.21(b) (1980) the NOAA has bestowed further head-aches on the councils by requiring councils to follow other federal statutes. For example, the National Environmental Policy Act (NEPA), 42 U.S.C. §§ 4321-4361 (1976) has been read by the NOAA to require a detailed environmental-impact statement for each fisheries-management plan. Federal Advisory Committee Act, 5 U.S.C. App., §§ 1-15 (1976), while only requiring "timely notice" of committee meetings, has been interpreted by NOAA to require fifteen days advance notice of council meetings. Executive order 12291 has forced councils to submit regulations to a rigorous economic analysis. The Paperwork Reduction Act and Regulatory Flexibility Act have also applied to the councils. As of December 1982, Congress was considering legislation that would exempt councils from the Federal Advisory Committee Act and further restrict the time frame for council plans.

68. 16 U.S.C.A. § 1854(c) (1) (A) (Supp. 1980).

69. Id. at § 1854(b) (2).

70. Id. at § 1855(a).

71. Id. at § 1855(b).

72. Id. at § 1855(c). Judicial review of the secretary's regulations is very limited. Id. at § 1855(d). A plaintiff must file for review within thirty days of the regulatory promulgation and may not enjoin enforcement of the regulations pending review. The Court is limited to ascertaining whether the regulations are "arbitrary or capricious" (without rational basis), which means regulations will almost always be upheld. See Comment, Judicial Review of Fishery Management Regulations under the Fishery Conservation and Management Act of 1976,

52 Wash. L. Rev. 599 (1977).

73. *Id.* at § 1853(a) (3), (a) (4) (A), (a) (4) (B), (a) (4) (C). The FCMA defines optimum yield as the amount of fish: "(A) which will provide the greatest overall benefit to the Nation, with particular reference to food production and recreational opportunities; and (B) which is prescribed as such on the basis of the maximum sustainable yield from such fishery, as modified by any relevant economic, social, or ecological factor." 16 U.S.C.A. § 1802(18) (Supp. 1980).

74. The NOAA has promulgated detailed data requirements under 50 C.F.R. § 602.3(b) (1980). *Id.* at § 602.3(b) (4)-(11), (14).

75. 16 U.S.C.A. § 1853(b) (Supp. 1980).

76. 16 U.S.C.A. § 1851 (Supp. 1980). For U.S.-Canada fisheries relations, the third national standard could prove to be the most important. The standard urges regional councils to cooperate with other jurisdictional authorities whenever a fish stock overlaps jurisdictional boundaries. Canada might use such a statutory duty as a keyhole to negotiation with the regional councils.

The importance of the duty to cooperate has been reemphasized in guidelines set by the secretary of commerce: "Unit of management, or at least cooperation between various jurisdictional authorities (e.g., State, Council, Federal Gov't), is vital to prevent jurisdictional disputes from adversely affecting conservation practices. Where management units cross Council or Federal-State boundaries, co-ordination should be sought among the several fisheries managers and Councils in the development of plans and regulations." 50 C.F.R. § 602.2(d) (2) (1980).

77. For possible conflicts of the MFCMA with a law-of-the-sea treaty, *see* Jacobson and Cameron, *Potential Conflicts between a Future Law of the Sea Treaty and the Fishery Conservation and Management Act of 1976,* 52 Wash. L. Rev. 451 (1977).

78. For a further summary of the various problems, *see* Comptroller General of the United States, *Progress and Problems of Fisheries Management Under the Fishery Conservation and Management Act* (Jan. 9, 1979) [hereinafter referred to as Comptroller General Report].

79. 16 U.S.C.A. § 1854(b) (Supp. 1980).

80. H.R. Rep. No. 94-445, 94th Cong., 1st sess., 10 (1975) *reprinted* in (1976) U.S. Code Cong. & Ad. News 631, S. Rep. No. 961, 94th Cong., 1st sess. (1975), *reprinted* in Legislative History, *supra* 33, at 736.

81. (1976) U.S. Code Cong. & Ad. News 675.

82. For example, concerning the status of councils, one congressman has stated: "They [councils] are fundamentally independent from the Secretary. They do not enjoy some degree of independence from the Secretary; they are basically, fundamentally and critically independent of the Secretary." Fishery Conservation and Management Act Oversight: Hearings before the House

Subcomm. on Fisheries and Wildlife Conservation and Environment of the Comm. on Merchant Marine and Fisheries, 96th Cong., 1st sess., 450 (1979) (statement of Congressman Studds) [hereinafter referred to as 1979 Oversight Hearings].

83. An example of such an abuse of power occurred in 1978 when the NMFS required fishermen to keep groundfish logbooks after the New England Council had voted against such a measure. National Fisherman, May 1980, at 7.

84. United States-Canada Fishing Agreements: Hearings before the House Subcomm. on Fisheries and Wildlife Conservation and the Environment of the Comm. on Merchant Marine and Fisheries, 96th Cong., 1st Sess., 133 (1979) (statement of Mr. Sharood).

85. 1979 Oversight Hearings, *supra* note 82, at 238 (statement of Richard N. Sharood). Cooperation between the councils and National Marine Service is, however, improving. Comptroller General Report, *supra* note 18, at 73.

86. 1979 Oversight Hearings, *supra* 82, at 439-440 (statement of Mr. Gordon). The legal opinions have tended to focus on language in the legislative history that indicated the Federal Advisory Committee Act would apply to all regional councils. (1976) Cong. Code & Ad. News 576.

87. The Federal Advisory Committee Act has been interpreted by NOAA to require fifteen days advance notice in the the *Federal Register* of committee meetings. 5 U.S.C. app. § 10 (1976). The Department of Commerce has added five more days for review and the NOAA another six days, so the total advance notice requirement is twenty-six days. Rogalski, *supra* note 67, at 195. As of December 1982 Congress was considering legislation that would exempt the councils from the Federal Advisory Committee Act. Councils are given forty-five days to make amendments to rejected plans. Twenty-six days would be taken up by the notice requirement, and even more time could be lost if advisory panels or statistical committees need to call a meeting. *Id.*

88. 1979 Oversight Hearings, *supra* note 82, at 442 (statement of Mr. Gordon). The NOAA is drawing up regulations to clarify the applicability of conflict-of-interest laws to the councils. U.S. Dept. of Commerce, *Calendar Year 1980 Report on the Implementation of the Magnuson Fishery and Conservation Act of 1976,* II-35 (March 1981) [hereinafter referred to as 1980 Calendar Report].

89. 1979 Oversight Hearings, *supra* note 82, at 788, 435, 449, 609.

90. *Id.* at 209 (chart submitted by James Walsh, deputy administrator, NOAA).

91. 1979 Oversight Hearings, *supra* note 82, at 842 (chart submitted by Langdon Warner, Environmental Defense Fund).

92. New England Fishery Management Council, *Interim Fishery Management Plan for Atlantic Groundfish* (September 30, 1981); New England Fishery Management Council, *Fishery Management Plan,* Final Environmental

Impact Statement, Regulatory Impact Review for Atlantic Sea Scallops (*Placopecten magellanicus*) 139 (January 1982); personal interview, Douglas Marshall, executive director, New England Fishery Management Council (July 16, 1982).

93. 1979 Oversight Hearings, *supra* note 82, at 992-994 (letter of Ronald E. Labisky, professor, fisheries and wildlife). The NMFS has awarded two contracts to assess social and economic factors as part of a five-year data-collection program and has initiated a national survey of recreational fishing. *Id.* at 175 (statement of James Walsh).

94. 1979 Oversight Hearing, *supra* note 82, at 503, 744. The secretary may issue emergency regulations for an initial forty-five-day period and may extend the regulations for another forty-five days. 16 U.S.C.A. § 1855(c) (Supp. 1980).

95. The twelve plans were: Atlantic groundfish and Atlantic herring (New England); surf clam and ocean quahog, Atlantic squid, Atlantic mackerel and butterfish (Mid-Atlantic); commercial and recreational salmon fisheries off the coasts of Washington, Oregon, and California, and northern anchovy (Pacific Council); tanner crab, groundfish of Gulf of Alaska, and high-seas salmon off the coast of Alaska (Northern Pacific); and Stone Crab of the Gulf of Mexico (Gulf of Mexico). 1980 Calendar Report, *supra* note 88, at 51-59. 45 C.F.R. 64996 (October 1, 1980), for groundfish. 45 C.F.R. 15957 (March 12, 1980), for herring. New England Fishery Management Council, *Fishery Management Plan, Final Environmental Impact Statement, Regulatory Impact Review for Atlantic Sea Scallops (Placopecten magellanicus)* (January 1982).

96. As an example, the New England Council's scallop plan integrates a plan, an impact statement, and a regulatory analysis into one document. *Id.*

97. 1980 Calendar Report, *supra* note 88, at 14. Congress could solve the problem as well. As of December 1982 Congress was considering legislation that would streamline the planning process.

The Mid-Atlantic Fishery Management Council is presently considering a framework plan for Atlantic mackerel, Loligo squid, Illex squid and Butterfish. The proposal, if approved would authorize the regional director of the National Marine Fisheries Service, in consultation with the Mid-Atlantic Council and after public comment, to vary optimum yields, domestic catches, and foreign catches according to existing provisions and criteria. Personal Interview, Salvatore A. Testeverde, National Marine Fisheries Service, Northeast Region (July 16, 1982).

98. For a summary of New England and Mid-Atlantic state laws concerning groundfish, *see* New England Fishery Management Council, *Interim Fishery Management Plan For Atlantic Groundfish* 47-48 (September 30, 1981). For a summary of scallop laws, *see* New England Fishery Management Council, *Fishery Management Plan, Final Environmental Impact Statement, Regulatory Impact Review For Atlantic Sea Scallops (Placopecten magellanicus)* 70 (January 1982).

99. 1979 Oversight Hearings, *supra* note 82, at 915 (statement of Mr. Eschwege). The same problem has plagued the Gulf Council's shrimp-management plan. A mass of rules and regulations have been ineffective since most of the critical events occur in state waters. National Fisherman, May 1981, at 5. The problem has been exacerbated by the MFCMA's lack of clarity as to when federal officials may preempt state power. Section 1856(b), which authorizes federal preemption for fisheries occurring predominantly in the 3- to 200-mile zone, fails to define *predominantly*. *Predominantly* could be defined by fish weight, fish value, the number of fishing vessels, or other criteria. Comptroller General Report, *supra* note 78, at 24.

Two approaches, however, could lessen the problem in the future. First, states might coordinate their fishing regulations with federal regulations. Innovative legislation in New Jersey and California shows just such a move. State enactments establish a state management system modeled after the federal system. That is, state councils will be responsible for formulating fisheries-management plans. The councils will be required to coordinate state plans with the appropriate regional council. See N.J. Stat. Ann. § § 23: 2B-1 to 2B-18 (West. Supp. 1980) and Cal. Fish & Game Code § § 7650-7653 (Supp. 1980). Second, regional councils might coordinate their plans with state plans or lack of plans. The New England Council's herring plan shows just such a move. Allowable catches of adult herring in the 3- to 200-mile zone are calibrated to the poundage of adult herring landed within state territorial waters. New England Fishery Management Council, *Amendment No. 3 to the Fishery Management Plan For The Atlantic Herring Fishery of The Northwest Atlantic*, 45 Fed. Reg. 15957, 15958 (March 12, 1980). Communication between federal and state officials is being facilitated by the State-Federal Relationship Program, which encourages meetings between State and Federal officials under the auspices of a cooperative agreement between the National Marine Fisheries Service and the Atlantic States Marine Fisheries Commission. Personal interview, Peter Colosi, Jr., National Marine Fisheries Service, Northeast Region (July 16, 1982).

100. 1979 Oversight Hearings, *supra* note 82, at 915 (statement of Mr. Eschwege). Recent cooperative enforcement agreements among coastal states, the NMFS, and Coast Guard may alleviate the problem. State agents are given authority to enforce federal regulations, and federal agents are given authority to enforce state regulation. In addition, there will be free exchange of enforcement personnel. 1980 Calendar Report, *supra* note 88, at 32-33.

101. 1979 Oversight Hearings, *supra* note 82, at 916 (statement of Mr. Eschwege).

102. *Id.* at 917.

103. *See, e.g., id.* at 177 (statement of James Walsh).

104. Hearing on the Fishery Conservation and Management Act of 1976, before the Senate Committee on Commerce, Science and Transportation, 95th Cong., 2d Sess., 66-67 (January 9, 1978) (statement of Thomas Jordon).

The Canadian Fisheries-Management System

The Canadian fisheries-management system is flexible and informal. Great administrative discretion allows federal officials to alter fishing regulations and policies almost overnight. Lack of a legislatively mandated consultation process allows officials to chart fishery-management policy virtually on the basis of plans of their own design, subject only to advice of their own choosing. Nevertheless, the system's contours may be discerned.

Constitutional Moorings

By its text, the Canadian Constitution appears to grant the federal government total control over the fisheries. Section 91(12) of the Constitution Act, 1867, crowns the federal Parliament with exclusive legislative authority over the sea and inland fisheries. However, judicial decisions, emphasizing provincial constitutional authority over property and civil rights, have opened the hatch for provinces to claim jurisdiction over those aspects of the fisheries where the property concept becomes central.[1] Two early cases, *The Queen* v. *Robertson* and *Attorney-General for Canada* v. *Attorney-General for Ontario, Quebec and Nova Scotia (the Fisheries Case),* made clear that only the provinces could issue leases granting exclusive fishing rights to nontidal lakes and streams, since the provinces retained a property interest and minor legislative competence over inland fisheries.[2] A later case, *Attorney-General for Canada* v. *Attorney-General for British Columbia (Fish Canneries),* expanded provincial power to encompass the licensing of fish curing and canning plants.[3] Lord Tomlin, in striking down the federal attempt to license provincial processing plants, suggested provincial powers might be quite broad once fish are captured and become property: "Trade processes by which fish when caught are converted into a commodity suitable to be placed upon the market cannot upon any reasonable principle of construction be brought within the scope of . . . sea coast and inland fisheries."[4] In a recent case, *Fowler* v. *The Queen,* the Supreme Court of Canada reiterated that federal fishing regulations may not overimpinge upon provincial property rights.[5] The Court found section 33(3) of the federal Fisheries Act, which prohibited placing logging debris into any waters, *ultra vires* the federal Parliament, for logging regulation came under provincial power over property and civil rights.[6]

The first two cases to address the question of federal-provincial power over fishing in tidal waters slammed the jurisdictional hatch shut on the provinces.

In *Attorney-General for British Columbia* v. *Attorney-General for Canada (British Columbia Fisheries Reference)*, the Privy Council declared that British Columbia retained no property interest, and thus no legislative competence, over tidal fisheries since under English common law, regardless of who owned the seabed, the public retained the right of fishing.[7] Viscount Haldane summarized the judicial reasoning succinctly:

> Neither in 1867 nor at the date when British Columbia became a member of Federation was fishing in tidal waters a matter of property. It was a right open equally to all the public, and therefore, when by S.91 sea coast and inland fisheries were placed under the exclusive legislative authority of the Dominion Parliament, there was in the case of the fishing in tidal waters nothing left within the domain of the Provincial Legislature. The right being a public one, . . . the exclusive power of regulation was placed in the Dominion Parliament.[8]

In *Attorney-General for Canada* v. *Attorney-General for Quebec (Quebec Fisheries)*, the Privy Council applied similar reasoning to defeat Quebec's claim for offshore fisheries jurisdiction. Their Lordships rejected Quebec's argument that old French law had granted the province property rights over tidal fisheries, since Quebec's preconfederation statutes had declared a public right to tidal fishing similar to English common law.[9]

Federal power over tidal fisheries was reemphasized in the recent case of *Northwest Falling Contractors Ltd.* v. *The Queen*.[10] There the Supreme Court of Canada upheld a federal prosecution under the Fisheries Act against a company that had spilled oil into a British Columbia ocean inlet. The Court rejected the defendant's argument that the subject of pollution fell under provincial property and civil rights power and found pollution regulation, so long as restricted to activities harmful to fish, to be *intra vires* the federal Parliament.

Although the *British Columbia Fisheries Reference* and *Quebec Fisheries* cases expressly closed the constitutional hatch on provincial jurisdiction over tidal fisheries, the provinces still retain two slight breathing spaces. First, since the maritime provinces have never conclusively contested federal jurisdiction over tidal fisheries, they still could argue, like Quebec, that old French law granted them a property interest in tidal fisheries. Support for this argument could be derived from *In Re Provincial Fisheries*, which indicated that the British crown acquired the rights and prerogatives previously belonging to the French king.[11] However, counterarguments are probably stronger. At least four cases suggest old law in the Maritimes is based upon English law. Allowance of a maritime claim to French law would create a judicial nightmare. Courts might often have to undertake the impossible task of determining whether a particular matter came under French or English jurisdiction and the almost-impossible chore of examining the rights of the French king in the eighteenth century.[12]

Second, the eastern provinces could argue for a property interest in, and thus legislative competence over, sedentary fisheries of the continential shelf such as scallops and oysters.[13] Such an argument might be anchored to three propositions. One, the Privy Council, in previous tidal cases, hinted that the provinces might retain a property interest in fisheries connected to the seabed:

> It will, of course, be understood that in speaking of this public right of fishing on tidal waters their Lordships do not refer in any way to fishing by kiddles, weirs, or other engines fixed to the soil. Such methods of fishing involve a use of the Solum which, according to English law, cannot be vested in the public, but must belong either to the Crown or to some private owner."[14]

Two, under international law, sedentary fishering ownership is tied to ownership of the continental shelf.[15] Three, the eastern provinces own the seabed off their coasts and therefore the sedentary species attached to the seabed.[16]

Even if the provincial claim were to be upheld, the practical effect over marine fisheries jurisdiction would be minimal. By analogy to the provincial property interest in inland fisheries, the provinces probably would have at the most the limited right to grant leases to sedentary fisheries and to govern the transfer of those leases. The federal government would still continue as the sole manager of ocean fisheries.

For some provinces the practical reality of fisheries management matches the constitutional reality. In New Brunswick, Nova Scotia, Prince Edward Island, and Newfoundland, the federal government continues to manage both the marine and freshwater fisheries. The provinces chip in by regulating the property aspects of the industry, such as processing, marketing, industrial development, and research.[17]

For other provinces the political knife has in practice sliced differently from the constitutional knife. In British Columbia, the province administers the freshwater fishery, while the federal government manages the marine and anadromous species. In Alberta, Saskatchewan, Manitoba, and Ontario, all fisheries are managed at the provincial level. In Quebec the province has been responsible for both marine and freshwater species.[18]

Such divisions of federal-provincial authority are, however, subject to substantial flux. For example, the federal government recently reestablished control over Quebec's marine fisheries because of Quebec's mismanagement.[19] As another example, the federal government recently granted Nova Scotia control over a $1 million freshwater fish hatchery and plans to turn over all trout regulation and enforcement to the province.[20]

In the late 1970s the eastern provinces cried loudly for a reshifting of fisheries management. Newfoundland, the most vocal, called for concurrent jurisdiction where the province would have the paramount voice about quota allocations in provincial waters. Nova Scotia, while initially supporting the New-foundland position, eventually grew worried over Newfoundland's possible intent to ban Nova Scotia fishermen from Newfoundland waters and finally joined New Brunswick and Prince Edward Island in advocating continued federal exclusivity but a more-effective consultation process.[21] Quebec argued for a greater voice in quota allocations and argued allocations based upon past catches, area con-tiguity, and provincial population size.[22]

In the 1980s, provincial cries over fisheries have quieted as attention has turned to an issue of greater immediate concern: ownership of offshore oil and gas. Newfoundland, wishing to control development of the offshore Hibernia oil field, has referred the ownership question to the Newfoundland Supreme Court. Ottawa has countered by sending the question to the Supreme Court of Ca-nada.[23] Brian Peckford, Newfoundland's premier, has engaged in an almost-daily verbal chafing of federal policy. Nova Scotia, desiring to control the potential natural-gas deposits on and around Sable Island, initially joined the political rhetoric but has subsequently set aside the ownership question by entering into a resource-sharing agreement with the federal government.[24]

If the Supreme Court of Canada decides in favor of Newfoundland's offshore claim, provincial clamorings over fisheries management, particularly sedentary-species management, could be renewed. If the Court favors the federal claim, provincial murmurs for offshore fisheries authority might be hushed for good.

Statutory and Regulatory Moorings

The statutes governing Canadian fisheries management may be grouped into four functional categories: organizational, jurisdictional, managerial, and promotional.

Organization

The organization of the Canadian fisheries-management bureaucracy has under-gone many statutory overhauls. In 1930 the old Department of Marine and Fisheries became the Department of Fisheries. In 1969 Canadian fishery man-agement became more fragmented when the new Department of Fisheries and Forestry was mandated to govern not only fisheries concerns but also forestry concerns. In 1971, because of a growing public demand for environmental pro-tection, fisheries management became even more fragmented by being trans-ferred to a new, multifaceted agency, the Department of the Environment in which the minister of the environment was also the minister of fisheries. Besides Fisheries and Forestry, the new department also included the Canadian Meteo-rological Service (from the Ministry of Transport), the Air Pollution Control

Division and the Public Health Engineering Division (from the Department of National Health and Welfare), the Water Sector (from the Department of Energy, Mines and Resources), the Canada Land Inventory (from the Department of Regional Economic Expansion), and the Canadian Wildlife Service (from the Department of Indian Affairs and Northern Development).[25]

Following criticisms from industry for delegating fisheries to such a low priority and following extension of fisheries jurisdiction to 200 miles, which created a severe need for greater national management, Parliament finally responded in 1979 by splitting the Department of the Environment into two, the Department of Fisheries and Oceans and the Department of the Environment.[26] The new minister of fisheries and oceans, of full cabinet rank, was given four specific mandates: to oversee seacoast and inland fisheries, to oversee fishing and recreational harbors, to oversee hydrography and marine sciences, and to coordinate Canada's ocean policies and programs.[27]

Jurisdiction

Canada's claims to offshore jurisdiction in order to protect fisheries may be viewed as a series of responses to international stimuli.[28] In the 1950s new foreign trawler fleets began to attack Atlantic fish stocks. The International Commission for Northeast Atlantic Fisheries (ICNAF), able only to recommend quotas and to rely on flagstate enforcement, was ineffectual. Law-of-the-sea conferences in 1958 and 1960 failed to resolve the width of the territorial sea or the nature of the adjacent fishing zone.[29] In response, Canada in 1964 enacted the Territorial Sea and Fishing Zones Act, which established a three-mile territorial sea and an adjacent nine-mile fishing zone.[30]

In late 1969 the S.S. *Manhattan,* a U.S. oil tanker, traversed the Northwest Passage and presaged the possibility of future environmental degradation of Arctic waters.[31] Canada responded by enacting the Arctic Waters Pollution Prevention Act, which declared a 100-mile "pollution zone" in Arctic waters in which Canada would strictly regulate shipping. As added insurance, Canada also declared a twelve-mile territorial sea, which would effectively close off the gateways to the Northwest Passage.[32]

In the early 1970s foreign trawler fleets continued their extensive overfishing. Although ICNAF attempted to harness the fleets by implementing national quotas in 1972, the effort failed since quotas tended to be set not on sound management principles but on the fishing capacity of the fleets.[33] By 1976, UNCLOS III negotiations, while favoring an economic zone concept whereby coastal states would have semisovereign rights over various ocean uses including fisheries, became bogged down.[34] Canada responded by unilaterally declaring, effective January 1, 1977, a 200-mile fishing zone adjacent to the Atlantic and Pacific coasts. On February 24, 1977, Canada completed the extension of fishing zones by implementing a 200-mile zone in Arctic waters.[35]

Mr. L.H. Legault, former alternate deputy representative to the Law of the Sea Conference, captured some of the Canadian sense of expectation over extended jurisdiction in his testimony before the House's Standing Committee on Fisheries and Forestry:

> With the extension of jurisdiction, we will not only do the surveillance, we will do the enforcement in the full sense of that term, apprehension and protection. . . . This is what will make surveillance and enforcement rather easier for us, and will bring this problem to manageable levels, because we will be able to control the number of vessels assigned to taking the quota we have allocated to a particular country. We will be able to control the fishing seasons and areas and so on; we will be able to require daily reporting of catch, daily reporting of position and so on. We will even be able, from time to time, to call on particular vessels because we are suspicious of their activities and . . . have them come to us.[36]

Management

Two statutes bear the brunt of managing Canadian fisheries. The Fisheries Act is the great source of managerial power over domestic fisheries. The Coastal Fisheries Protection Act is the key source of managerial authority over foreign fishing.[37]

Rather than fleshing out numerous fishing regulations in detail, the Fisheries Act dangles three bare hooks waiting to be baited with administrative discretion. Section 7 allows the minister of fisheries and oceans "in his absolute discretion" to issue fishing leases and licenses. Section 33 forbids the disposal of deleterious substances into water frequented by fish but leaves to cabinet discretion what should be deemed deleterious. Section 34 grants the Canadian cabinet discretion to regulate in thirteen areas:

1. Proper management of seacoast and inland fisheries.
2. Conservation and protection of fish.
3. Catching, loading, landing, handling, transporting, and disposing of fish.
4. Operation of fishing vessels.
5. Use of fishing gear and equipment.
6. Issuing and cancelling of fishing licenses and leases.
7. Conditions of licenses or leases.[38]
8. Obstruction or pollution of any waters frequented by fish.
9. Conservation of spawning grounds.
10. Export of fish.
11. Interprovincial transport or trade of fish.
12. Duties of federal employees.
13. Delegation to federal administrators to vary any close time or fishing quota.

The Coastal Fisheries Protection Act authorizes the Canadian cabinet to control the conditions under which foreign fishing vessels may enter Canadian fisheries and authorizes protection officers to board and search fishing vessels in Canadian waters.[39] Pursuant to the act, Cabinet has issued regulations restricting such matters as mesh sizes, area closures, and species quotas.[40]

Promotion

Four statutes grant the fishing industry direct financial assistance. The Fisheries Development Act authorizes the minister of fisheries and oceans to develop new fisheries, new products, better efficiency, better vessels and equipment, and better handling, processing, and distributing.[41] Actual regulations pursuant to the act offer industry 50 percent of the cost (up to $50,000) to better fish chilling, such as the refrigerated parts of vessels, a third of the cost (up to $150,000) to better commercial cold storage or bait freezing facilities, and a 35 percent cost subsidy for the construction or modification of seacoast vessels over twenty-five feet or inland vessels over sixteen feet.[42] The Fisheries Improvement Loans Act offers fishermen guaranteed loans to improve fishing vessels, equipment, and shore installations.[43] The Fisheries Prices Support Act authorizes a Fisheries Prices Support Board to either purchase fish at prices set by it or to pay fishermen the difference between a price set by the board and the actual market price.[44] The Saltfish Act authorizes the Canadian Saltfish Corporation to assist the saltcod industry by buying and selling cured or uncured fish, by marketing and exporting saltfish, and by providing loans to fishermen and producers.[45]

Other statutes, although not specifically aimed at fisheries, also lend financial support. For example, fishermen often rely on the Unemployment Insurance Act for financial support during the offseason. Fishermen also receive special tax breaks such as the right to average incomes over a five-year span to reduce the tax on fluctuating incomes.[46]

Administrative Moorings

The actual administrative workings of the Department of Fisheries and Oceans may be summarized under two major headings: administrative organization and administrative plan-making procedures.

Administrative Organization

The Department of Fisheries and Oceans consists of four main organizational components: Atlantic Fisheries, Pacific and Freshwater Fisheries, Economic

Development and Marketing, and Ocean Science and Surveys.[47] Atlantic Fisheries, responsible for fisheries management on the East Coast, not only has key staff located in Ottawa but also has three regional offices, which carry on the bulk of management activity. The Newfoundland Region oversees fisheries in Newfoundland and Labrador, the Gulf Region manages the Gulf of St. Lawrence, and the Scotia-Fundy Region covers Georges Bank, the Bay of Fundy, and the Scotian Shelf. Pacific and Freshwater Fisheries, responsible for fisheries management in central and western Canada, is similar in structure. Although some key personnel are located in Ottawa, the majority are located in three regional offices: the Ontario Region, the Western Region (Prairie Provinces and Northwest Territories), and the Pacific Region (British Columbia and Yukon). Economic Development and Marketing, stationed in Ottawa, has four main functions: promotion of fish marketing, development of economic data and policy, administration of financial-assistance programs such as Fishing Vessel Assistance and Fisheries Improvement Loans, and negotiation concerning international fisheries relations. Ocean Science and Surveys, responsible for oceanographic and hydrographic programs, operates through four regional science centers: the Bedford Institute of Oceanography (Dartmouth, Nova Scotia), the Champlain Centre for Marine Science and Surveys (Quebec, Quebec), the Bayfield Laboratory for Marine Science and Surveys (Burlington, Ontario), and the Institute of Ocean Sciences (Sidney, British Columbia). Governing all four sectors of the federal bureaucracy are the minister of fisheries and oceans and his deputy (figure 3-1).

The Scotia-Fundy Region, certain to be of central importance to any U.S.-Canadian joint management scheme on the East Coast, displays a structure similar to other regions. The region is headed by a director general who oversees seven branches: the Field Operations Branch (responsible for actual fisheries management), the Fisheries Development Branch (responsible for development of fishing technology), the Small Craft Harbours Branch (responsible for administering harbor facilities), the Resource Branch (responsible for scientific research and biological advice on fish stocks), the Economics Branch (responsible for economic studies and program development), the Management Services Branch (responsible for internal services such as record keeping and accounting), and the Personnel Branch (responsible for staff oversight).[48] Each branch has its own individual director.

The branch with the largest staff, greatest budget, and prime responsibility for fisheries management is the Field Operations Branch, which operates through four divisions. The Conservation and Protection Division licenses both domestic and foreign vessels and administers surveillance and enforcement. The Inspection Division monitors products, plants, and vessels for health safety and undertakes various scientific studies related to product quality, storage, and handling. The Fishermen's Services Division manages federal-assistance programs such as Fishing Vessel Insurance and Fishing Vessel Subsidy Programs. The Resource

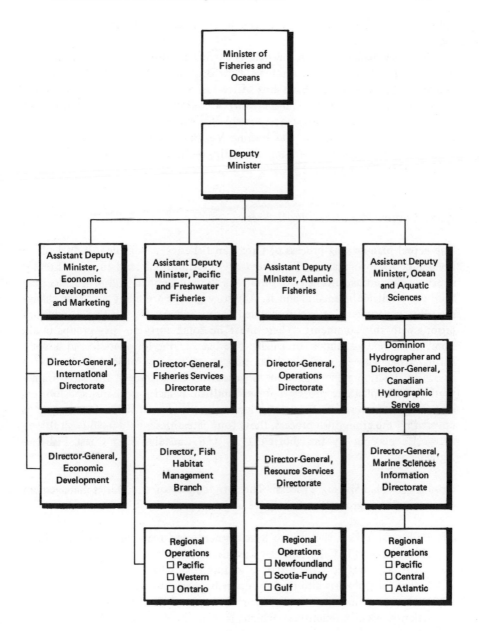

Source: Modified from Dept. Fisheries and Oceans, *Annual Report 1979–80* 26 (1981).

Figure 3-1. Organization of Department of Fisheries and Oceans

Allocation Division advises and assists in formulation of quota management plans.

Fisheries management in the field is carried on through the offices of three area managers located in St. Andrews, New Brunswick, Yarmouth, Nova Scotia, and Sydney, Nova Scotia. Each area office has an inspection chief (responsible for quality control and plant inspection), a conservation chief (responsible for enforcement), a project officer (responsible for supervising various projects such as Fishing Vessel Insurance and Fishing Vessel Subsidy Programs), and community-service officers (responsible for acting as liaisons between fishermen and government). (See figure 3-2.)

Administrative Plan-Making Procedures

The actual plan-making process of Canadian fisheries management is difficult to document for two reasons. First, advisory contributions tend to evade literary capture. Numerous informal consultations with fishermen and processors may take place outside normal channels. Advisory groups are many and ever changing. One government official responded to my request for a listing of advisory groups with this comment: "There must be some forty to fifty groups in all. Some come and go, almost overnight. I've been trying for years to pin down a listing. When you get one, please let me know." Second, official publication is sparse in describing the management process.[49] Nevertheless, the basic frameworks of the planning processes for groundfish, pelagics, scallops, and lobsters may be pieced together from interviews with various officials. Since squid is covered by the groundfish process, these four categories would include all fifteen categories covered by the aborted 1979 U.S.-Canadian East Coast Fisheries Agreement.

Groundfish Plan-Making Process: The production of a fisheries-management plan for Atlantic groundfish has twelve major steps:[50]

1. Biological advice, such as stock assessments and recommended total allowable catches (TACs), from the Canadian Atlantic Fisheries Scientific Advisory Committee (CAFSAC), a committee which moulds advice from individual biologists into final products by peer review.
2. Review by the Atlantic Director Generals Committee, (also called the Atlantic DGS Committee) which is composed of five directors-general (the three regional directors from Scotia-Fundy, Newfoundland and the Gulf and two directors from Ottawa) and two assistant deputy ministers (Atlantic Fisheries and Economic Development and Marketing).
3. Preparation of a draft management plan by the Atlantic Groundfish Advisory Committee Working Group, composed of nine federal officials

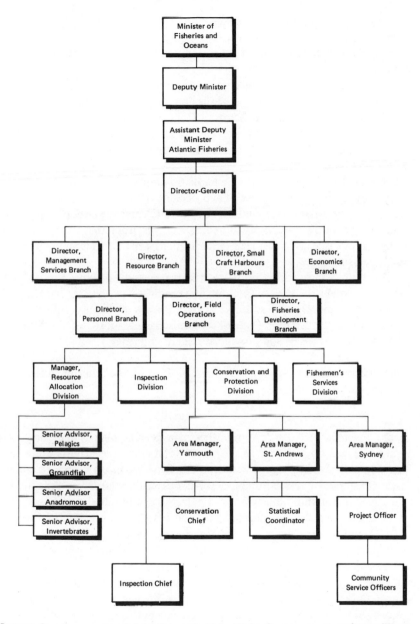

Source: Based on personal interview with R.J. Allain, former manager of surveillance and enforcement, Department of Fisheries and Oceans, Scotia-Fundy Region (November 4, 1982), and Greg Peacock, senior advisor on pelagics, Department of Fisheries and Oceans, Scotia-Fundy Region (June 22, 1982).

Figure 3-2.   Organization of the Scotia-Fundy Region

(a chairperson, two fisheries management personnel from each east coast region and two officials from Ottawa).

4. Review of the draft management plan by the Atlantic Director Generals Committee.
5. Additional consultations between the Atlantic Groundfish Advisory Committee Working Group and the fishing industry (Formal industry groups—the Scotia Fundy Groundfish Advisory Committee and the Gulf Groundfish Advisory Committee—have formed to facilitate the process).
6. Possible draft revision by the Atlantic Groundfish Advisory Committee Working Group.
7. Review by the Atlantic Director Generals Committee.
8. Review by the minister of fisheries and oceans.
9. Review by the Atlantic Groundfish Advisory Committee (AGAC), an interregional committee composed of representatives from the Department of Fisheries and Oceans, provincial fisheries departments, fishermen's groups, and processor groups.
10. Review by provincial fisheries officials in two possible forums—the Federal-Provincial Atlantic Fisheries Committee (composed of the Deputy Minister of Fisheries and Oceans and East Coast provincial deputy ministers of fisheries) and the Atlantic Council of Ministers (composed of the Minister of Fisheries and Oceans and provincial fisheries ministers).
11. Final draft revision.
12. Announcement of the Atlantic Groundfish Plan by the minister of fisheries and oceans.

Under the present Atlantic groundfish management plan, some forty-two stocks are managed on a quota basis. That is, total allowable catches are established for domestic and foreign fisheries.[51] The Canadian catch is divided among five basic categories of vessels: under sixty-five feet in length/fixed gear, under sixty-five feet in length/mobile gear, sixty-five to one hundred feet/fixed gear, sixty-five to one hundred feet mobile gear, and vessels over one hundred feet in length.[52] Overall quotas for the various vessel classes are set pursuant to the planning process. According to a concept called sector management, implemented in January 1982, inshore fishermen (vessels under sixty-five feet) may fish only in their regional sector and actual management (for example, actual division of quotas among fixed and mobile gears) would be discretionary with the regional director general. According to a concept called enterprise (or company) allocation, implemented on an experimental basis in 1982, the four major fish-processing companies (National Sea Products Ltd., H.B. Nickerson and Sons, The Lake Group, and Fisheries Products) are granted individual quotas to be caught when and how they desire.

Total allowable catches theoretically are supposed to be set to encompass social, economic, political, and environmental factors.[53] In practice, TACs have tended to be set conservatively in order to rebuild fish stocks.[54]

Pelagic Plan-Making Process: Each of the three East Coast regions—Gulf, Scotia-Fundy, and Newfoundland—manages small pelagics independently, and each has its own advisory committee structure.[55] This section deals only with the Scotia-Fundy regional management process since that process could be central to any U.S.-Canadian joint management in the future. Because mackerel, an under-utilized species, is not under quota management, this section further narrows consideration to the herring management process.

The production of a fisheries-management plan for herring has eight major steps:

1. Biological advice from the Canadian Atlantic Fisheries Scientific Advisory Committee (CAFSAC).
2. Review by the Atlantic Director Generals Committee.
3. Preparation of a draft management plan by the Resource Allocation Division of the Field Operations Branch.
4. Review by Scotia-Fundy Working Groups (S.W. Nova and Cape Breton), consisting of representatives from Fisheries and Oceans, provincial fisheries, and fishermen's groups.
5. Possible draft revision by the Resource Allocation Division of the Field Operations Branch.
6. Review by Scotia-Fundy director general.
7. Review by two Herring Advisory Committees (the Scotia-Fundy Herring Advisory Committee and the Ad Hoc Purse Seine Committee).[56]
8. Final review by the Resource Allocation Division and the Scotia-Fundy director general.

Scallop and Lobster Planning Processes: Since neither scallops or lobsters are under strict quota management and since regulations have tended to be more stable than for groundfish or herring, the planning processes for scallops and lobsters are much more rudimentary and less formalized.[57] No yearly management plans are issued. Instead regulatory and policy reviews occur as needed.

For scallops, the typical review process may have six steps:

1. Advice from CAFSAC on stock condition and recommendations for maximizing catch poundage.
2. Review by the Scotia-Fundy director general.
3. Review by a federal working group and possible draft of regulatory changes.
4. Review by the director general.

5. Consultation with advisory groups, either the Offshore Scallop Advisory Committee or the Bay of Fundy Scallop Advisory Committee.
6. Approval of any regulatory changes by the director general or further consultation by the director general with the assistant deputy minister of Atlantic fisheries.

Review of lobster regulations and policies is undertaken by the Scotia-Fundy Lobster Management Committee, composed of federal officials. Although considering the formation of a formal advisory committee of fishermen and processors, the Department of Fisheries and Oceans consults with fishermen informally through field biologists and area managers.

Practice

After Canada extended offshore jurisdiction to 200 miles on January 1, 1977, fishermen and processors applauded. With the phase-out of foreign competition, all expected their gumboots to become lined with gold. While fish stocks have recovered under extensive national management since 1977, fishermen and processors have not been so fortunate. Today they find themselves in economic hardship as serious as ever.[58] Many small processors have fallen to bankruptcy. Large processors tend to operate in the red.[59] Fishermen still tend to have low incomes and still tend to rely on unemployment insurance.[60]

Accusatory fingers are usually pointed at one or more of five problems: harvesting overcapacity, processing overcapacity, seasonality, quality, and marketing. (A further five problems also trouble the industry and managers: lack of fisherman participation in management decisions, lack of scientific knowledge, lack of enforcement, regulatory overcomplexity, and regulatory changes that occur without sufficient notice or consultation.) Combined, the five major problems are producing an economic whirlpool, threatening to sink the industry.

Harvesting Overcapacity

From 1976 to 1981 the number of fishermen in Atlantic Canada jumped from approximately 40,000 to 60,000, and the number of vessels increased from approximately 29,000 to 34,000.[61] Too many fishermen and boats for too few fish has resulted in a serious harvesting overcapacity.

The causes for such a situation are at least five in number. First is the common property nature of the resource. Free access to wild fish stocks, requiring no feeding, no payment of property taxes as in agriculture, and only a minimal investment in equipment has invited fleet growth. Since the first captor wins the fins, a vicious circle of competition is created. Fishermen are forced to keep increasing their harvesting capabilities (for example, by buying new sonar or a bigger engine) to keep up with the "other guy." More fishermen with greater technology, chasing the same number of fish, spells economic losses for all.[62] Second, a high unemployment rate and a lack of alternative employment has made the fishing industry a great sponge for jobless workers. Third, governmental financing, such as the federal Fishing Vessel Assistance Program, has enticed fishermen to acquire newer and bigger boats. Fourth, banks and credit unions, ecstatic over the security and profitability promised by the extension of offshore jurisdiction to 200 miles, gladly financed fishing boats and gear. Fifth, politicians have tended to facilitate license issuance as electoral enticements around election time. For example, just prior to a recent election, political influence more than doubled the number of crab licenses in Nova Scotia.[63]

Four remedial steps have already been undertaken by the Department of Fisheries and Oceans. In June 1980, the department placed an overall freeze on the expansion of personal fishing licenses for Atlantic fishermen.[64] The offshore groundfish fleet can grow no larger than current size and may acquire factory and freezer vessels (under two hundred feet in length) only to replace existing trawlers and only to catch underutilized species.[65] Marketing and quality control are in the process of being upgraded to increase economic viability. Experimentation with granting individual property shares to companies or fishermen's associations has been initiated in three fisheries: offshore groundfish, Bay of Fundy herring, and Labrador shrimp.[66] Other remedial steps could also be taken in the future. For example, the department could expand license buy-back programs or could extend individual catch quotas to individual fishermen.[67]

Processing Overcapacity

From 1976 to 1981 the number of processing plants in Atlantic Canada soared from 519 to approximately 700. Too many plants for too few fish has resulted in many plant shutdowns and many worker layoffs.[68]

The causes for such a situation are at least three in number. Financial institutions, expecting greater offshore jurisdiction to result in greater industrial profits, willingly loaned money to processors. The Federal Department of Regional Economic Expansion (DREE), created to pump new economic life into disadvantaged regions, bestowed grants for new processing facilities based more on political considerations than on the availability of fish stocks.[69] Provinces, having jurisdiction over plant licensing, issued licenses freely since increased processing promised increased employment.

Seasonality

Inshore vessels tend to have a short fishing season, approximately from April through October, since fall and winter bring stormy weather and offshore fish migrations. The resultant glut of fish during the warm-weather season causes economic problems. The flooded market tends to depress fish prices. Processors may have to store excess fish until the market is ready, which invokes high storage costs. Some small processors may be forced to lie idle during the off-season.

The problem of seasonality is exacerbated by the Department of Fisheries and Oceans's express policy to favor inshore fishermen in quota allocations.[70] If the department favors the offshore fleet, which can harvest on a year-round basis, and thereby lessens the seasonal glut, the inshore fleet will catch less and suffer financially. If the department favors the inshore fleet, the seasonality problem grows and the offshore fleet loses economically. To find a balance between inshore and offshore demands continues to be a thorny issue for federal managers. A partial solution to the seasonality problem would be to ship fish caught offshore by truck or boat to small seasonal plants to reduce shutdowns during the inshore's offseason.[71]

Quality

Although 70 to 80 percent of Canada's fish products are of high quality, some 20 to 30 percent may be of poor or inconsistent quality, which arguably has resulted in lower prices for Canadian fish.[72] Blame for the quality problem rests with poor handling by both processors and fishermen, particularly the inshore fishermen.[73] The small-boat operators tend not to have adequate room for refrigeration and storage boxes, tend not to bleed or gut fish at sea, tend to store fish at depths over three feet, and tend to handle fish with forks or suction pumps.[74]

To counter such quality problems, the Department of Fisheries and Oceans is considering an expansion of quality regulations to require vessel certificates (for adequate storing and chilling equipment) and a maximum fish-storage depth of three feet.[75] The Task Force on Atlantic Fisheries recently identified four options to upgrade quality: mandatory gutting and icing at sea, dockside grading by government-certified industry buyers, a port market authority that would purchase all fish at prices related to quality and thereafter sell the fish to processors, and final product grading.[76] Thus, some changes in quality regulations will probably occur within the near future.

Marketing

Two marketing problems appear to plague the Canadian fishing industy at the present time. Fragmented marketing—too many individual Canadian processors selling fish in foreign markets—has caused unnecessary interdomestic competition, which has driven foreign prices down.[77] Overdependence on the U.S. fish market, where consumer demand is down and where foreign competition is up, has forced Canadian processors to hold large inventories.[78]

To counter these marketing problems, the Department of Fisheries and Oceans has approved some over-the-side sales (direct sales by fishermen to foreign vessels), has negotiated lower foreign tariffs on Canadian fish exports in exchange for foreign access to Canadian fish stocks, has undertaken numerous marketing studies, and may initiate an export licensing system that would limit export to the most proficient.[79] Other possible solutions, such as a crown corporation to market Canadian seafood, are likely to be suggested by the Task Force on Atlantic Fisheries.[80]

Notes

1. Constitution Act, 1867, S. 92(13). For the text of the Act, *see* 30 & 31 Victoria, c. 3 (U.K.) or R.S.C. 1970, Appendices, pp. 191–238.

2. (1882) 6 S.C.R. 52, [1898] A.C. 700 (P.C.).

3. [1930] A.C. 111, [1929] 3 W.W.R. 449, [1930] 1 D.L.R. 194 (P.C. 1929].

4. *Id.* at 121. Provincial power over trade processes, such as processing and marketing, is not without limits. Lord Tomlin noted that if the federal government had shown plant licensing to be of "national importance" and to "have attained such dimensions as to affect the body politic of the Dominion," then federal regulation would have been upheld. *Id.* at 122. Also, processing and marketing, insofar as such functions involve interprovincial or international trade, may invoke federal jurisdiction over trade and commerce. Constitution Act, 1867, S. 91(2). For a discussion of the federal trade and commerce power, *see* P.W. Hogg, *Constitutional Law of Canada* 267–274 (1977).

5. [1980] 32 N.R. 230, *reversing* [1979] 1 W.W.R. 285, 45 C.C.C. 2d 161, 93 D.L.R. 3d 724, *which aff'd* [1977] 4 W.W.R. 449, 36 C.C.C. 2d 297, *which rev'd* 6 W.W.R. 28 (S.C.C.).

6. 32 N.R. at 241. The decision seemed to hinge on two major rationales. First, the federal government had failed to show timber debris to have a specific deleterious effect on fish. *Id.* Second, section 33(3) was overbroad. It specified no standard concerning the amount of debris; it covered not only water frequented by fish but water flowing into such water; and it, in fact, covered the whole spectrum of logging operations. *Id.* at 243. For provincial cases upholding federal environmental regulation under the Fisheries Act, *see Attorney-General of Canada* v. *Aluminum Co. of Canada Ltd.,* [1980] 115 D.L.R. 3d 495 and *The Queen* v. *Forest Protection Ltd.,* [1978] 20 N.B.R. 2d 653, 34 A.P.R. 653, 7 C.E.L.R. 93, *Leave to appeal to S.C.C. dismissed, sub. nom. The Queen* v. *Forest Protection Ltd., Forest Protection Ltd.* v. *Concerned Parents Group Inc.,* [1979] 29 N.B.R. 2d 270 n., 66 A.P.R. 270 n., 29 N.R. 533 (S.C.C.).

7. [1914] A.C. 153, 15 D.L.R. 308 (P.C. 1913). The Privy Council avoided answering the ownership question since ownership was irrelevant to

the decision and a question of international law. *Id.* at 174, 15 D.L.R. at 319.

8. *Id.* at 172, 15 D.L.R. at 317–318.

9. [1921] 1 A.C. 413, 56 D.L.R. 358, (P.C. 1920); *id.* at 423, 56 D.L.R. at 362–363.

10. [1980] 32 N.R. 541, 2 S.C.R. 292: R.S.C. 1970, C. F-14; 32 N.R. at 550, 2 S.C.R. at 301.

11. [1895], 26 S.C.R. 444. *Also see Dixson* v. *Snetsinger* [1872], 23 U.C.C.P. 235. For a general discussion of these cases, *see* G. LaForest, *Natural Resources and Public Property Under the Canadian Constitution* 8 (1969).

12. For a listing of the cases and an expansion of the arguments, *see id.* at 9.

13. For an excellent summation of the provincial arguments, *see* Fairley, *Canadian Federalism, Fisheries and the Constitution: External Constraints on Internal Ordering,* 12 Ottawa L. Rev. 257, 284–289 (1980).

14. *British Columbia Fisheries Reference,* [1914] A.C. at 167, 15 D.L.R. at 314.

15. 1958 Geneva Convention on the Continental Shelf, art, 2, para. 2, 499 U.N.T.S. 314.

16. In *Reference Re Ownership of Offshore Mineral Rights,* [1967] S.C.R. 792, 65 D.L.R. 2d 353, the Supreme Court declared the federal government owned the seabed off British Columbia. The Court based its decision on three principles. First, British Columbia never claimed or acquired ownership over the seabed either before or after confederation. *Id.* at 808, 65 D.L.R. 2d at 367. Second, offshore mineral resources are a matter of national concern and therefore enter the field of federal jurisdiction under the initial words of the BNA Act S. 91 "the peace, order and good government of Canada." *Id.* at 817, 65 D.L.R. 2d at 376. Third, the federal government is the sovereign responsible for international relations, of which the offshore forms a key part. *Id.* at 821, 65 D.L.R. 2d at 380.

Since the Court has never ruled upon offshore ownership on the East Coast, the eastern provinces may argue historical distinctions from the British Columbia case. For a review of provincial arguments, *see* G. LaForest, *Water Law in Canada: The Atlantic Provinces* 463-468 (1973), Harrison, *The Offshore Mineral Resources Agreement in the Maritime Provinces,* 4 Dalhousie L.J. 245 (1978), LaForest, *Canadian Inland Waters of the Atlantic Provinces and the Bay of Fundy Incident,* 1 *Can. Yearbook Int. L.* 149 (1963), and Foley, *Nova Scotia's Case for Coastal and Offshore Resources,* 13 Ottawa L. Rev. 281 (1981). For a general discussion of the unsettled nature of offshore claims, *see* Harrison, *Jurisdiction over the Canadian Offshore: A Sea of Confusion,* 17 Osgoode L.J. 469 (1979).

17. Maritime Ocean Resources Ltd., *The Canadian Fisheries and Ocean Industries Directory* 277 (1981). [hereafter referred to as Canadian Ocean Directory] ; *see, e.g.,* Province of Nova Scotia, *16th Annual Report, Department of Fisheries* (1980).

18. Canadian Ocean Directory, *supra* note 17, at 277. Fishery regulations of all the provinces, however, are enacted as federal regulations. *See* C.R.C.,

1978, Vol. VII, chapters 838 (Alberta Fishery Regulations), 840 (British Columbia), 843 (Manitoba), 844 (New Brunswick), 846 (Newfoundland) and C.R.C. 1978, Vol. VIII, chapters 847 (N.W. Territories), 848 (Nova Scotia), 849 (Ontario), 850 (P.E.I.), 852 (Quebec), 853 (Saskatchewan) and 854 (Yukon).

Quebec's greater autonomy over the fisheries has probably stemmed from two factors. First, the federal government, historically, had few francophones or French-speaking anglophones in the public service; thus French-speaking provincial managers could more effectively administer the regulations. E.P. Weeks and A. Sommerville, *The Future of the Atlantic Fisheries* 16 (1982). Second, under a 1922 agreement, the federal government delegated managerial responsibilities to Quebec since Quebec fishermen limited their fishing almost entirely to coastal waters and used only stationary equipment. Minutes of the House of Commons Standing Committee on Fisheries and Forestry, 1st sess., 32d Parliament, Issue No. 46, at 20 (March 25, 1982) (Statement of Mr. LeBlanc, Minister of Fisheries and Oceans).

19. Federal regulations were extended to cover Quebec's commercial fishing in the Gulf of St. Lawrence for scallops, shrimp, herring, or groundfish by means of mobile gear and for groundfish by means of fixed gear from vessels over thirty-five feet in length. Atlantic Fishing Registration and Licensing Regulations, amendment, S.O.R./82-283, *Canada Gazette* 998-999 (March 24, 1982). Quebec failed to forward statistics to the Federal Department of Fisheries and Oceans, allowed fleet expansion against federal advice, and even forbid non-Quebec residents from fishing in the Quebec zone. Minutes of the House Standing Committee on Fisheries and Forestry, 1st sess., 32d Parliament, Issue No. 46, at 20 (March 25, 1982) (Statement of Mr. LeBlanc, Minister of Fisheries and Oceans).

20. Halifax Chronicle-Herald, June 10, 1982, at 10.

21. S. Dunn, S. McCorquodale, and A.P. Pross, *East Coast Fisheries: Constitutional Issues in Newfoundland* 11-13, 14 (unpublished manuscript, Dalhousie University, 1981).

22. Such principles would have doubled Quebec's harvests. Weeks and Sommerville, *supra* note 18, at 16-17.

23. The possibility still exists, however, for a negotiated settlement. Federal Energy minister Jean Chretien has renewed negotiations over the offshore with Newfoundland Energy Minister William Marshall. *See* Halifax Chronicle Herald, December 11, 1982, at 4.

24. The agreement, effective regardless of any future court decisions, provides for a federal-provincial regulatory board and detailed revenue sharing. For an extensive summary of the agreement, *see* Halifax Chronicle-Herald, March 5, 1982, at 8-10.

25. The Department of Fisheries Act, S.C. 1930, C. 21; Government Organization Act, 1969, S.C. 1968-69, C. 28; Government Organization Act, 1970, S.C. 1970-71-72, Vol 1, C. 42. D.M. Johnston, *The Administration of Canadian Fisheries,* 22-23 (unpublished manuscript, Dalhousie Law School, April, 1978).

26. Government Organization Act, 1979, S.C. 1978-79, C. 13.

27. To assist the minister in marine-science oversight, Parliament also established the Fisheries and Oceans Research Advisory Council, a group of twenty-four scientists to advise on such matters as fisheries research and fisheries programs, in place of the old Fisheries Research Board. *Id.* at pt. II, pt. I, para 5.

28. For a detailed treatment of Canada's maritime claims, *see* L.H.J. Legault, "Maritime Claims," *in Canadian Perspectives on International Law and Organization* 377-397 (MacDonald, Morris, and Johnston, eds., 1974). Of course, there were domestic stimuli as well. For example, in 1963 the Fisheries Council of Canada, a national federation of regional industry associations, submitted an influential brief to the Canadian Parliament calling for the establishment of an offshore fishing zone. F. Redding, *Sharing the Living Resources of the Sea: An Analysis of Contemporary American-Canadian Fisheries Relations* 168-169 (Ph.D. thesis, Univ. of Oklahoma, 1979).

29. For a summary of the ill-fated law of the sea negotiations, *see* B. Johnson, "Canadian Foreign Policy and Fisheries," 61-64 in *Canadian Foreign Policy and the Law of the Sea* (Johnson and Zacher, eds., 1977).

30. S.C. 1964, C. 22. The act also authorized the use of straight baselines for measuring the territorial sea. Fishing vessels of Britain, Portugal, Spain, Italy, Norway, and Denmark were allowed to continue fishing off the East Coast pending phase-out negotiations. The United States and France were allowed to continue fishing pursuant to former treaty rights. In practical effect, then, the contiguous fishing zone only prevented additional countries from joining the fishery. B. Johnson, *supra* note 29, at 66.

31. *Id.* at 70.

32. R.S.C. 1970 (1st Supp.), C. 2. Territorial Sea and Fishing Zones Act, amendments, R.S.C. 1970, C. T-7. Pursuant to the act, the Canadian cabinet also declared three exclusive fishing zones: the Gulf of St. Lawrence (zone 1), the Bay of Fundy (zone 2), and Queen Charlotte Sound, Hectate Strait, Dixon Entrance (zone 3). Fishing Zones of Canada (Zones 1, 2, 3) Order, C.R.C. 1978, Vol. XVIII, C. 1547, p. 13739.

33. Johnston, *Legal and Diplomatic Developments in the Northwest Atlantic Fisheries,* 4 Dalhousie L.J. 37, 45 (1977). [hereafter referred to as Legal and Diplomatic Developments] ; paper presented by Brian Rothschild at the 16th Law of the Sea Institute Conference, Dalhousie University (June 23, 1982). A lack of quota enforcement also hampered the management effort. Personal communication, Department of Fisheries and Oceans official.

34. Legal and Diplomatic Developments, *supra* note 33, at 46.

35. Fishing Zones of Canada (zones 4 and 5) Order, C.R.C. 1978, Vol. XVIII, C. 1548, p. 13741; Fishing Zones of Canada (zone 6) Order, C.R.C. 1978, Vol. XVIII, C. 1549, p. 13747.

36. Minutes of the Proceedings of the House of Commons Standing Committee on Fisheries and Forestry, 1st Sess., 30th Parliament, Issue No. 71, at 40 (May 27, 1976).

37. R.S.C. 1970, C. F-14; R.S.C. 1970, C. C-21.

38. This provision is probably the major fountainhead for fisheries regulations. Essentially all fisheries are now subject to limited entry; that is, fishermen must acquire a fishing license from the Department of Fisheries and Oceans. *See* Atlantic Fishing Registration and Licensing Regulations, C.R.C. 1978, Vol. VII, C. 808, pp. 5051–5056. Such licenses may restrict fishing as to area, species, amount, and gear. *See* SOR/80-792, *Canada Gazette* p. 1507 (May 14, 1980).

39. R.S.C. 1970, C. C-21, SS. 3-4, 5.

40. *See* Foreign Vessel Fishing Regulations, C.R.C. 1978, Vol. VII, C. 815, p. 5083, *as amended.* Of course, the authority to issue foreign regulations would also arise from section 34(g) of the Fisheries Act.

41. R.S.C. 1970, C. F-21.

42. Fish Chilling Assistance Regulations, C.R.C. 1978, Vol. VIII, C. 861, p. 5905, *as amended.* Fishery Products Storage Regulations, C.R.C. 1978, Vol. VIII, C. 862, p. 5909, *as amended.* Fishing Vessel Assistance Regulations, C.R.C. 1978, Vol. VIII, C. 863, p. 5913, *as amended.* Pursuant to the Fishing Vessel Assistance Program, Fisheries and Oceans granted $8,490,661 in subsidies for the construction of 548 fishing vessels (324 on the Atlantic coast) during the 1980–1981 fiscal year. Dept. Fisheries and Oceans, *Annual Report 1980-81* 17 (1982).

43. R.S.C. 1970, C. F-22. For the actual regulations, *see* Fisheries Improvement Loans Regulations, C.R.C. 1978, Vol. VIII, C. 864, p. 5917, *as amended.* During the 1980–1981 fiscal year, the Department of Fisheries and Oceans administered some 1,158 loans, amounting to $23.2 million. Dept. Fisheries and Oceans, *Annual Report 1980-81* 16 (1982).

44. R.S.C. 1970, C. F-23. Due to favorable market conditions, no deficiency or price-stabilization programs were authorized during the 1980–1981 fiscal year. Dept. Fisheries and Oceans, *Annual Report 1980-81* 17 (1982).

45. R.S.C. 1970 (1st Supp.), C. 37.

46. R.S.C. 1970, C. U-2 is the Unemployment Insurance Act. In 1979 unemployment benefits to Maritime and Newfoundland fishermen totaled $52,326,000. E.P. Weeks and A. Sommerville, *The Future of the Atlantic Fisheries* 50 (1982). For a detailed listing of the various tax breaks, *see* A. Scott and P. Neher (eds.) *The Public Regulation of Commercial Fisheries in Canada* 60 (1981).

47. Dept. Fisheries and Oceans, *Canada's Department of Fisheries and Oceans* (1981).

48. For a detailed account of branch programs and branch subdivisions, see Dept. Fisheries and Oceans, *Annual Report 1980, Maritimes Region* (1981).

49. Only a skeletal overview is provided by Departmental publications. *See, for example,* Dept. Fisheries and Oceans, *Policy for Canada's Atlantic Fisheries in the 1980's* 55-58 (1981). Although the Atlantic Fisheries Resource Management Process has been cited as a publication available upon request, as of July 1982, no such publication was available. *See id.* at 61.

50. Based on personal interviews with Nancy Dale, chairperson of the Atlantic Groundfish Advisory Committee Working Group, Department of Fisheries and Oceans, Scotia-Fundy Region (June 16, 1982), Cheryl Fraser, statistical officer of quotas, Department of Fisheries and Oceans, Scotia-Fundy Region (August 3, 1982), and David Bollivar, manager fleet services and strategy, National Sea Products Ltd., Halifax, Nova Scotia (June 9, 1982).

51. Foreign fishing is limited to two situations: where there is a surplus to Canadian harvesting capacity and where there are special circumstances such as agreement by foreign countries to lower tariff rates in return for access to the Canadian zone or agreement by a foreign country to restrict fishing of stocks straddling Canada's 200-mile zone in return for access to the Canadian zone. As an example of a tariff-access agreement, Canada has agreed to grant the European Economic Community (EEC) access to cod and squid in exchange for lower EEC tariffs on Canadian fish. *See* Halifax Chronicle-Herald, October 27, 1981, at 8. As an example of a conservation-access agreement, Canada has negotiated a treaty with Spain that would grant Spain access to Canadian cod and squid in exchange for Spanish agreement to restrict fishing on the Grand Banks beyond Canada's 200-mile zone. *See* Halifax Chronicle-Herald, June 23, 1982, at 4. The treaty, however, has not been signed and is facing stiff political opposition. Personal interview, Bob Prier, chief of Conservation and Protection Division, Department of Fisheries and Oceans, Scotia-Fundy Region (August 3, 1982).

52. For the actual quota regulations, *see* Atlantic Fishery Regulations, amendment, SOR/82-195, *Canada Gazette* pp. 648-675 (Feb. 10, 1982).

53. Such an approach is often referred to by various terminologies, for example, "best use," "optimal social-economic benefit," or "optimum sustainable benefit." *See* Dept. Fisheries and Oceans, *Policy for Canada's Atlantic Fisheries in the 1980's* 6 (1981) and S. Dirlam, *New England-Canadian Maritime Provinces Fisheries Management Workshop Summary* 6 (Workshop held at University of Rhode Island, May 12-13, 1978).

54. Canada has tended to set quotas at the F 0.1 level, which is generally 10 to 20 percent below maximum sustainable yield. Dept. Fisheries and Oceans, *Policy for Canada's Atlantic Fisheries in the 1980's* (i) (1981). Of course, F 0.1 arguably takes account of socioeconomic factors; that is, it may be socially and economically beneficial to rebuild fish stocks. For a discussion of the various strategies in setting harvest levels, *see id.* at 8-17. For the scientific definition of F 0.1 *see* J.A. Gulland, *The Concept of the Marginal Yield from Exploited Fish Stocks,* 32 J. Cons Per. Intl. Explor. Mer. 256-261 (1968), and J.A. Gulland and L.K. Boerema, *Scientific Advice on Catch Levels,* 71 Fishery Bulletin 325-335 (1973).

55. Based on personal interviews with Greg Peacock, senior adviser on pelagics, Department of Fisheries and Oceans, Scotia-Fundy Region (June 22, 1982), and Roger Stirling, executive director, Seafood Producers Association of Nova Scotia, Dartmouth, Nova Scotia (June 15, 1982).

Management of large pelagics is beyond the scope of this book. Suffice it to say, Bluefin Tuna is managed primarily by the International Commission for the Conservation of Atlantic Tuna. Actual division of the Canadian Total Allowable Catch (TAC), set by the Commission, is carried out by federal officials in consultation with an interregional advisory committee (the Atlantic Bluefin Advisory Committee). A Swordfish Plan is developed by federal officials using CAFSAC recommendations on the TAC and considering advice from a Swordfish Advisory Committee (centered in the Scotia-Fundy region). Personal Interview, Bob Prier, chief of the Conservation and Protection Division, Department of Fisheries and Oceans, Scotia-Fundy Region (August 3, 1982).

56. The Scotia-Fundy Herring Adivisory Committee is composed of representatives from DFO, provincial fisheries, processors, and fishermen's groups. The Ad Hoc Purse Seine Committee is composed of three representatives from each of the three purse-seiner associations—the Atlantic Herring Fishermen's Marketing Co-operative, Southwest Seiners Ltd., and Gulf Seiners). The Ad Hoc Purse Seine Committee, chaired by the Scotia-Fundy director-general, was formed in April 1981 to address the special problems of the purse-seine fleet (approximately sixty-six vessels) and holds numerous meetings to discuss such issues as seiner quotas and a possible buy-back program. The Scotia-Fundy Herring Advisory Committee operates primarily through the Working Group level, having representatives on the Working Groups and making recommendations as to Working Group membership. Thus, the Advisory Committee tends to be more an informational forum than an advisory forum.

57. Based upon personal interviews with R. Crouter, director-general, Department of Fisheries and Oceans, Scotia-Fundy Region (July 20, 1982); J.D. Pringle, head of the crustaceans and marine plants section within the Invertebrates and Marine Plants Division, Resource Branch, Department of Fisheries and Oceans, Scotia-Fundy Region (August 4, 1982); and Greg Stevens, officer of regulation and enforcement policy, Fisheries Operations Branch, Department of Fisheries and Oceans, Scotia-Fundy Region (August 4, 1982).

Offshore scallop catches are presently harvested under a number of restrictions including: limited entry; a meat count of forty scallops per pound; twelve-day trip limit; 30,000 pound maximum catch per trip; and 180,000 pound maximum limit for each of the four-month periods April to July, August to November, and December to March. See *Atlantic Fishery Regulations,* CRC 1978 Vol. VII, C.807, as amended. Although overall quotas (total allowable catches) were set for Georges Bank in 1982 for both inshore and offshore vessels, they are administrative in nature and designed to give the department flexibility through the use of variation orders, if required. The actual management of fishing activities continues to be through the enforcement of meat counts, twelve-day trip limits, and trip quotas.

Lobster catches are regulated in five ways: limited entry, season limit, size limit, trap limit, and a ban on taking egg-bearing females. Lobster Fishery Regulations, C.R.C. 1978, Vol. VII, C. 817, *as amended*. Special provisions apply to Browns Bank (400,000-pound annual quota for all vessels and area closure) and Georges Bank (no quota).

58. The hardship is so serious that the federal cabinet has established two task forces to study and make recommendations concerning federal fisheries policy. The task forces are the Commission on Pacific Fisheries Policy, headed by Peter H. Pearse and usually referred to as the Pearse Commission, and the Task Force on Atlantic Fisheries, headed by Michael Kirby and usually referred to as the Kirby Task Force. The Pearse Commission issued a preliminary report, "Conflict and Opportunity Toward a New Policy for Canada's Pacific Fisheries," in October, 1981. The Kirby Task Force submitted its report to cabinet in the fall of 1982. The report should be made public in early 1983.

59. For example, in 1981 National Sea Products Ltd. lost $1,682,000 from fishing operations. Although the first six months of 1982 showed a small profit, a loss is expected in the third quarter. Halifax Chronicle-Herald, August 6, 1982, at 4-F. The Nickerson firm reportedly owes creditors in excess of $100 million. Halifax Chronicle-Herald, May 26, 1982, at 3.

60. Approximately 90 percent of Atlantic fishermen averaged a yearly income of roughly $7,800 in 1979. E.P. Weeks and A. Sommerville, *The Future of the Atlantic Fisheries* 22-23 (1982).

61. Halifax Chronicle-Herald, January 16, 1982, at 7.

62. For a more-detailed description of the common-property problem, *see* W. Hale and D. Wiltusen, *World Fisheries: A "Tragedy of the Commons"?* (1970).

63. J.B. Morrow, "National Fisheries Policy: The Perspective of Industry," *Canada and the Sea* 95, 98 (The Association for Canadian Studies, Spring 1980).

64. Weeks and Sommerville, *supra* note 18, at 32.

65. Dept. Fisheries and Oceans, *Policy for Canada's Atlantic Fisheries in the 1980's* iii (1981).

66. Halifax Chronicle-Herald, February 12, 1982, at 7; C.R. Levelton, *Toward an Atlantic Coast Commercial Fisheries Licensing System* 35 (1981).

67. Buy-back schemes have been used in the Atlantic lobster and Pacific salmon fisheries. Two recent Economic Council of Canada studies make a recommendation for individual quotas. *See* Economic Council of Canada, *Reforming Regulation* 1981 69-79 (1981), and A. Scott and P. Neher (eds.), *The Public Regulation of Commerical Fisheries in Canada* 41-49 (1981).

68. Halifax Chronicle-Herald, January 16, 1982, at 7; *id.*, February 23, 1982, at 10-F (Plant Closure Shatters Fishermen's Dream).

69. J.B. Morrow, "National Fisheries Policy: The Perspective of Industry," *printed in Canada and the Sea* 95, 98 (Association for Canadian Studies, Spring 1980).

70. *See* Dept. Fisheries and Oceans, *Policy for Canada's Atlantic Fisheries in the 1980's* 5 (1981). This policy of favoring the inshore, however, has not

been totally consistent in practice. For example, in 1979 the haddock TAC for the Scotia-Fundy region was 62 percent (inshore) and 38 percent (offshore). In 1982 the offshore was allocated just over 50 percent of the haddock catch. Halifax Chronicle-Herald, March 23, 1982, at 22. For a listing of offshore groundfish quotas, see R.D.S. MacDonald, "Fisheries Policy and the Development of Atlantic Coast Groundfisheries Management," in Fisheries Decision-Making in Canada: Perspectives on East Coast Policy-Setting and Implementation (to be published by Dalhousie Ocean Studies Programme). For a general discussion of governmental favoritism to the offshore fleet, see J. Jansen, Regional Socio-Economic Development: The Case of Fishing in Atlantic Canada 203-212 (Ph.D. Thesis, Rutgers University, 1981).

71. Newfoundland has initiated such a program, E.P. Weeks. Key Issues Facing the East Coast Fisheries of Canada 19-21 (1979).

72. Percentages extracted from a speech of Coline Campbell, Member of Parliament, S.W. Nova, at the National Conference on the Future of the Atlantic Fisheries (Halifax, Nova Scotia, June 3, 1982). For arguments that factors other than quality, such as depressed markets, high interest rates and excess harvesting/processing capacity, are responsible for economic woes, see D. MacDonald and L. Mazany, An Economic Analysis of Quality Improvement and Marketing Issues in the Atlantic Fishery (Paper prepared for the National Conference on the Future of the Atlantic Fisheries, June 3, 1982) [hereafter referred to as MacDonald and Mazany].

73. Canadian Fishing Report, July 1982, at 17 (statement of Michael Kirby).

74. Dept. Fisheries and Oceans, Policy for Canada's Atlantic Fisheries in the 1980's 49-50 (1981).

75. Id. at 49-52.

76. Task Force on Atlantic Fisheries, Issues and Options 10-11 (July 13, 1982).

77. Halifax Chronicle-Herald, February 23, 1982, at 14. For arguments that fragmented marketing may not be a serious problem, see MacDonald and Mazany, supra note 72.

78. Approximately 60 percent of Atlantic foreign fish sales go to the United States. Weeks and Sommerville, supra note 18, at 43.

79. Current policy permits such over-the-side sales in two situations: where catches are surplus to domestic processing capacity and where Canadian fishermen cannot sell to Canadian processors at an acceptable economic return. Dept. Fisheries and Oceans, Policy for Canada's Atlantic Fisheries in the 1980s 28 (1981). In 1982 over-the-side sales were approved for herring, mackerel, gaspereaux, and cod (West Coast of Newfoundland). Fisheries Council of Canada Bulletin, June 1982, at 6-7.

80. For the marketing options identified by the task force, see Task Force on Atlantic Fisheries, Issues and Options 11-15 (July 13, 1982).

East Coast Fisheries Agreement of 1979

Overview of the Agreement

On March 29, 1979, Canadian Ambassador Peter Towe and U.S. Secretary of State Cyrus Vance signed a combined boundary treaty and fishery agreement covering the Gulf of Maine and Georges Bank. (The boundary treaty required the parties to submit the boundary dispute to the International Court of Justice or, if not agreeable to both parties, to a court of arbitration.) The fishery agreement, the result of nearly two years of negotiation by Marcel Cadieux of Canada and Lloyd Cutler of the United States, was intended to be an insurance policy to guarantee joint management and reciprocal fishing rights no matter where the boundary line would eventually be drawn.[1] The agreement would have established a joint East Coast Fisheries Commission, having eight members from each country, which would have managed three categories of fish stocks.[2] A stocks would have been managed jointly with an equal voice for each side.[3] B stocks would have been managed by the country with primary interest subject to review by the other country.[4] C stocks would have been managed by only one country with consultation with the other country.[5] Any unresolvable disputes over management measures for A and B stocks would have been subject to binding arbitration.[6]

While the Joint Commission was to determine the overall yearly catch for each fish stock, the agreement cemented the percentages that each country would receive. For example, Canada was to receive 73.35 percent of the scallop catch while the United States received 26.65 percent. As a trade-off, the United States would have received the majority of groundfish (83 percent of cod, 79 percent of haddock, and 90 percent of silver and red hake). Another major trade-off would have given Canadians the right to fish for 9 percent of the Loligo squid in U.S. waters in exchange for the U.S. right to fish for redfish in Canadian waters, an agreement that would have terminated in ten years.[7]

Although the agreements were deposited with the U.S. Senate on April 18, 1979, the first Senate hearings were not held until April 15, 1980.[8] Heavy political opposition bogged down any ratification of the fishery agreement, and on March 6, 1981, President Reagan killed the agreement by withdrawing it from the Senate.[9] Since then both countries have agreed to send the boundary dispute to a Chamber of the International Court of Justice.[10]

Reasons for Nonratification

At least ten factors contributed to the demise of the 1979 fisheries agreement.

Natural Delays

Protracted debates by the Senate on strategic-arms limitation and protracted preparation of an environmental-impact statement by the State Department combined to delay hearings for nearly a year, which gave political foes time to organize and gather forces.[11]

U.S. Presidential Election

President Carter and his administration, the agreement's prime supporters, backed off in pushing the agreement so as not to alienate the political support of New Englanders.[12]

Strong New England Fishing Industry Lobby

A powerful lobby group, the American Fisheries Defense Committee, was formed for the sole purpose of defeating the fishery agreement. The committee claimed to represent 90 percent of the organizations involved in commercial fisheries on the East Coast and brandished some very influential persons. Alan Guimond, the executive director, had served on the advisory panel to the U.S.-Canada fishing negotiations. Leigh Ratiner, counsel and Washington representative, was an old Washington hand and former member of the U.S. negotiating team to UNCLOS III.[13]

Fear of Subverting the New England Council

Although the State Department pledged to appoint three New England Council members and two Mid-Atlantic Council members to the Joint Commission, many opponents of the fishery agreement feared the Joint Commission would usurp management powers of the councils.[14] They also feared that many management decisions eventually would be made by a third-party arbitrator.[15]

Fear of a New Layer of Regulations

The U.S. fishing industry, not caring for any form of regulation, feared a whole new layer of international regulations would be added to already-burdensome national and state regulations. Such apprehension was expressed before the House of Representatives on behalf of the American Fisheries Defense Committee:

> The bilateral Commission will inevitably double the bureaucratic complexity facing FCMA implementation today, because it will constitute a totally separate and additional level of decision-making necessary before management actions can be taken. The result will not only impede the healthy and efficient development of the American commercial fishing effort but may also frustrate the achievement of desireable conservation objectives.[16]

Belief the Scallop Allotment Was Inequitable to the United States

The 73.35:26.25 percent scallop allotment in favor of Canada was based on the average national harvests for the years 1964 through 1976. Many opponents of the fishery agreement felt such figures were unfair since Canada had heavily subsidized its fishing fleet during those years and since the United States historically had harvested a much greater percentage of scallops (91 percent in 1957 and 100 percent before 1950).[17]

Dislike for the Redfish-Loligo Squid Trade-Off

Under the fishery agreement Maine fishermen would have gained access to Canadian redfish, while Canadian fishermen would have gained access to Loligo squid off the mid-Atlantic coast of the United States. New Jersey fishermen and New Jersey Congressman William Hughes strongly opposed any giveaway of "southern" stocks for the sole benefit of a "northern" state and feared Canadian squid catches from U.S. waters might eventually compete in American markets.[18]

Willingness by U.S. Fishermen to Gamble

U.S. fishermen displayed a great willingness to gamble, for two reasons. First, U.S. fishermen knew they could at the worst lose only one-third of Georges Bank, but at the best they could gain the whole bank. Second, U.S. fishermen had the security of alternative employment.[19]

Belief in the U.S. Legal Position

Many U.S. officials, believing in the eventual victory of the U.S. boundary claim, viewed the 1979 fishery agreement not as an insurance policy in case of losing the boundary dispute but as a permanent shackle binding the United

States to give away American fish.[20] Their belief in the U.S. legal position was fed by a U.S. law review article that interpreted the U.S. position favorably:

> It has been concluded that . . . the North Sea Continental Shelf cases opinion can only be a decided asset to the United States in Atlantic continental shelf talks or arbitration with Canada. It has been concluded that the American rather than the Canadian stance on Atlantic delimitation is likely to be the more successful in any potential adjudication of the controversy.[21]

Belief in the Indestructibility of the Scallop Resource

Many U.S. officials believed a fishery agreement could wait until after the boundary settlement since industry economics would guarantee the health of fish stocks. That is, if fish became scarce, many fishermen would go out of business and the stocks would revive.

Such a view was expressed by Senator Claiborne Pell:

> Even if the proper conservation practices are not followed for the next few years as these negotiations go on and the scallops become more rare, is it not a fact that the normal process of regeneration eventually will occur? After all, as the scallops become more rare, it will become uneconomic to fish for them. Then a period of years will go by during which the stocks will regenerate.
>
> So, I don't think we should get too worried about letting a little time go by. We should approach it in exactly the way President Reagan has recommended, by decoupling it. Maybe 2, 3 or 4 years from now we can go after the other problem.[22]

Notes

1. For the text of the agreement, *see* U.S. Dept. of State, *Draft Environmental Impact Statement on the Agreement between the United States and Canada on East Coast Fisheries Resources, Appendices,* Appendix 1 (March, 1980) [hereinafter referred to as U.S.-Canada East Coast Fisheries Agreement].

2. Appointment of seven members would have been left to national discretion. The eighth member for each country would have required joint approval and would have acted as a co-chairperson of the commission. *Id.* at 2.

3. A stocks include pollock, mackerel, cusk (Georges Bank stock), and lobster (Gulf of Maine-Georges Bank). *Id.* at 50–54 (Annex A). The treaty only mandated that the commission set a total allowable catch for each fish stock. Other management measures, such as mesh size or incidental catch, would have been discretionary. *Id.* at 27–29. Lobsters would have been jointly managed

only until a boundary decision. *Id.* at 54. Mackerel, while requiring a joint decision on total allowable catch, would have been managed individually by each country in its own waters. *Id.* at 51.

4. B stocks include Atlantic herring (excepting juveniles within three miles of the coastline), scallops (Georges Bank), cod (Georges Bank), haddock (Georges Bank-Gulf of Maine), silver and red hakes (Georges Bank), argentine, white hake, and Illex squid. *Id.* at 55–66 (Annex B). Management measures, proposed by the country designated as having the primary interest in the fishery, would have become binding if consistent with governing principles such as "optimum yield" and "best scientific information available." *Id.* at 13-16. For scallops, each country would have set a total allowable catch for its own allocated jurisdiction. Other management measures, such as shell size and meat count, would have been decided jointly (as for A stocks). *Id.* at 60-61.

5. C stocks include cod (Scotian Shelf-Gulf of Maine), haddock (Scotian Shelf), redfish, Loligo squid, lobster (after boundary delimitation), and other groundfish. *Id.* at 67-78. Consultations would have had to precede management implementation (except for conservation emergencies) and would have had to comply with governing principles such as "optimum yield" and "best scientific evidence available." *Id.* at 16.

6. Commission decisions would have always been subject to review by the parties, a term left undefined by the treaty. *Id.* at 12, 14. While each government could have thereby chosen its own internal review process, each country apparently contemplated review by selected federal officials. Personal interview, David Bollivar, former associate director, International Fisheries Relations Branch, Department of Fisheries and the Environment, present manager of Fleet Services and Strategy, National Sea Products Ltd. (August 10, 1982). If federal officials could not resolve management issues, decision making would have passed to the two co-chairpersons of the Joint Commission. In case of disagreement there, an arbitrator would have made a binding decision. The arbitrator would have been appointed by joint agreement. In case of disagreement, the president of the International Court of Justice would have been required to appoint an arbitrator who was not a national or resident of the United States or Canada. U.S.-Canada East Coast Fisheries Agreement, *supra* note 1, at 38-41.

7. *Id.* at 60, 61–63, 73–74, 78.

8. Wang, *Canada-United States Fisheries and Maritime Boundary Negotiations: Diplomacy in Deep Water,* 38/39 Behind the Headlines 1, 30 (1981).

9. Hearing on the Maritime Boundary Settlement Treaty with Canada before the Senate Committee on Foreign Relations, 97th Cong., 1st sess., 2-3 (March 18, 1981) (Letter of President Reagan) [hereinafter referred to as Treaty Hearing, 1981]. For a further discussion of the agreement *see* D. Bollivar, *Canada/United States East Coast Fisheries Treaty—An Overview* (Paper presented to the Halifax Branch of the Canadian Institute of International Affairs, January 22, 1981).

10. For a discussion of the adjudication, *see* Note, *International Adjudication: Settlement of the United States—Canada Maritime Boundary Dispute,* 23 Harv. Intl. L.J. 138 (1982).

11. Wang, *supra* note 8, at 31.

12. *Id.*

13. *Ocean Science News,* April 16, 1979, at 1. Two members of the five-person executive council, Jacob Dykstra and Alan Guimond, were members of the New England Council.

14. Hearings on United States-Canadian Fishing Agreements before the House Subcommittee on Fisheries and Wildlife Conservation and the Environment of the Committee on Merchant Marine and Fisheries, 96th Cong., 1st sess., 46 (June 22, 1979) (Prepared Statement of Mr. Lloyd Cutler) [hereinafter referred to as 1979 Fishing Agreement Hearings].

15. *Id.* at 136 (Statement of Mr. Sharood).

16. *Id.* at 27 (Statement of Leigh Ratiner).

17. *Id.* at 27 (Statement of Congressman Studds).

18. *Id.* at 74 (Statement of Congressman Hughes).

19. Wang, *supra* note 8, at 43.

20. Review of entitlements could have taken place every ten years, but in case of arbitration, a party could not lose during the first review more than 5 to 10 percent of its annual commercial catch. In subsequent reviews, a party could not lose more than one-third of its original entitlement. U.S.-Canada East Coast Fisheries Agreement, *supra* note 1, at 22-24.

21. 1979 Fishing Agreement Hearings, *supra* note 14, at 69 (Statement by Leigh Ratiner).

22. Treaty Hearing 1981, *supra* note 9, at 13 (Statement of Senator Pell).

Options

Once the International Court of Justice draws a boundary line in the Gulf of Maine-Georges Bank region, numerous possibilities will exist for U.S.-Canadian fisheries relations. At one extreme, the boundary could act as a great barrier reef where each country, having little or no desire for joint management, would individually supervise its own local lagoon.[1] At the other extreme, the boundary could act as a connective bridge, perhaps resurrecting the 1979 East Coast Fisheries Agreement, with just minor modifications, and perhaps easing treaty passage through the U.S. Senate.[2]

This chapter assumes neither scenario will occur. That is, the United States and Canada will both wish for some form of joint management, but the required two-thirds U.S. Senate vote for treaties will still lurk as a great tidal wave, waiting to be unleashed by local lobbies who disfavor regulated fisheries or foreign concessions.[3] Such an assumption may not be far-fetched if one listens to the lessons of history or the rhetoric of Canadian officials.

The history of U.S.-British and Canadian fisheries relations shows that the U.S. Senate has upset numerous treaties. In 1888 the United States and Britain signed a treaty, usually referred to as the second Treaty of Washington or the Bayard-Chamberlain Treaty, clarifying U.S. access to Canadian East Coast waters and reinstituting free trade in fish products, which might have resolved over one hundred years of tumultuous conflicts.[4] Instead the U.S. Senate, having a Republican majority that was unwilling to give President Cleveland, a Democrat, an advantage in an impending election, defeated the treaty in a strict party vote. Not one Republican voted for the treaty; not one Democrat voted against.[5] In 1902 the U.S. and Newfoundland negotiated a treaty, the Bond-Hay Agreement, which would have granted American fishermen access to Newfoundland bait and supplies in exchange for U.S. removal of customs duties on certain fish products. The Senate refused to ratify the agreement after New England processors, heavy contributors to the Republican cause, opposed any lowering of protective tariffs.[6] A 1920 Pacific salmon treaty, signed by the United States and Britain, was never reported from the Senate Committee on Foreign Relations.[7] A 1929 salmon treaty was defeated by the Senate.[8] In 1930 the United States and Canada signed a revised salmon treaty, but the U.S. Senate delayed ratification seven years until Canada accepted three new amendments.[9] In 1923 the United States and Canada signed a halibut treaty, the first treaty ever concluded independently by Canada. Because the treaty covered only American and Canadian fishermen, the U.S. Senate decided to amend the convention to cover all British nationals. Only after Canada refused did the Senate retract and ratify.[10]

Canadian officials have often pointed out the destructive potential of the Senate ratification procedure. Tony Campbell, director general of Fisheries and Oceans' International Directorate, when asked about the chances for a U.S.-Canada tuna agreement, responded, "It is clear that the American government seriously wishes for an agreement, but we cannot rely on the Senate. I can say that the American government is quite serious, but there are always doubts concerning the Senate."[11]

Mr. L.H. Legault, director general of the Bureau of Legal Affairs and legal adviser for external affairs, spoke this way:

> But I think you know something about the workings of the U.S. Senate. Where an issue affects in particular a given region, the senators from that region have virtually a right of veto on how the issue will be determined; and of course, if anyone breaks the rules of the club, then when a reciprocal sort of treatment is being sought by the senator who broke ranks, he does not get that kind of co-operation in return. That is the way the system works.[12]

Mark MacGuigan, secretary of state for external affairs, reacting to Senate behavior in delaying the 1979 fisheries agreement, stated:

> The Canadian side must patiently await the U.S. Senate's "Take-it-or-leave-it" proposals for amendment to a treaty which was concluded only after long and difficult negotiations. Clearly, this is not acceptable. Clearly, differences in approaches to foreign policy here reach a point where rational management of a crucial bilateral relationship may no longer be possible.[13]

How, then, may the United States and Canada cooperate in future fisheries management without the Senate's upsetting all efforts? What form should their cooperation take? Three cooperative bridges, each able to better withstand rough political seas than the sunken 1979 agreement, are possible.

First, the United States and Canada could enter into a treaty agreement, as in 1979, but a treaty with major renovation to remove political stress points. Such an approach might be described as the *causeway* since it is the most formal and requires the heavy cement of Senate approval. Second, both countries could enter into an executive agreement, which might be labeled the *suspension bridge,* since it is much less formal and would not require the undermooring of Senate ratification. Third, both countries could avoid any formal agreement in favor of informal consultations. Such an approach might be called the *pontoon bridge,* since consultative bridges would be deployed and retrieved, as needed.

Treaty Approach

If the United States and Canada choose to link their management systems by a treaty, they will face two major structural choices. They could be aggressive and design an elaborate management regime, modified from 1979, complete with administrative arrangements, such as a joint commission, and distributive provisions, detailing how transboundary stocks are to be apportioned between the two countries. Such an agreement may be referred to as an administrative-distributive treaty. Or they could be more tentative and less elaborate by merely agreeing on general management principles and pledging to bolster consultation and coordination. Such an agreement may be labeled a demonstrative treaty (that is, demonstrating cooperative intentions).[14]

Much can be said in favor of a demonstrative treaty rather than an administrative-distributive agreement for the Gulf of Maine–Georges Bank region. National management systems are still in early adolescence, open to experimentation and change. For example, Canada is experimenting with company quotas, which could eventually be extended to individual fishermen. The United States is experimenting with deregulation of the groundfish industry, which could eventually lead to a new Atlantic demersal finfish plan. A tight administrative-distributive treaty might stunt national experimentations or might soon be outgrown. A demonstrative treaty with general principles of cooperation, however, would perhaps allow the opportunity for both countries' management systems to mature, while still coaxing coordination. National regimes are also extremely divergent at the present time. Canada favors limited entry and strict quota management, while the United States favors free access and no quota management (at least as to groundfish). An administrative-distributive treaty might be like forcing two incompatible animals—an eagle and a beaver, in this case—into a single burlap bag. One would expect great screeching and eventually, a torn bag. A demonstrative treaty would perhaps allow a gradual and gentle adaptation of differing management philosophies through mutual consultations.

On the negative side, the general principles of a demonstrative treaty could hinder joint management. Officials, not forced to reach concrete decisions according to a set administrative framework, might be encouraged to engage in abundant international talk but little cooperative action.

If the United States and Canada choose an administrative-distributive type causeway, they should seriously consider modifying the three most-troublesome piers of the 1979 agreement—resource allocation, institutional set-up, and dispute settlement—to defuse at least partially political opposition.

Resource Allocation

The allocation in the 1979 agreement of exact fish stock percentages to each country was perhaps a fatal flaw. U.S. scallop fishermen, angry over a mere

26.65 percent allotment, and U.S. squid fishermen, enraged over granting Canadians 9 percent of American Loligo squid, raised their political voices and helped drown the agreement.

There are two basic reasons for allocation's being such a politically sensitive area. First the act of allocation by its very nature tends to create winners and losers. Those who believe they received a good deal may celebrate. Those convinced they received a raw deal are almost certain to protest. Second, the principles of allocation are still rather unsettled in international law. While the overall principle of equity has gradually emerged as the way to divide shared resources between two or more states,[15] there is still no consensus on what such a principle means in practice.[16] Nations still tend to disagree on how much weight to give to specific allocative factors such as geographic distribution of fish stocks, economic dependency, historical use, and managerial ability.

L.H. Legault, director general of the Bureau of Legal Affairs and legal adviser, External Affairs Canada, recently summed up the amorphous nature of equity: "At this moment . . . this notion of equity is a very difficult one. Some people say that equity corresponds to the length of the chancellor's foot. I would say that equity is in the eye of the beholder."[17]

Given these two major difficulties—the creation of losers and the unsettled nature of international law—Canada and the United States would be wise not to specify exact allocations in a future treaty. To do so would tend to drag out negotiations and tend to incite special-interest groups to lobby against treaty ratification.

Instead the two countries should delegate actual allocation decision making to an institution created by the treaty to carry on joint management.[18] Such a move would have at least two advantages. First, political opposition would be delayed until after Senate ratification, when losers would not crash upon elected, vulnerable senators but would beat against the buffer of an appointed administrative body. Second, the malleable nature of equity would be better recognized. Equity is incapable of being frozen, for national needs and desires tend to vary from year to year. For example, development of Sable Island gas off Nova Scotia might entice fishermen into alternative employments and thereby lessen Canadian fishing capacity. An administrative body, evaluating national allocations on a yearly basis, could adjust and account for such a variation; a preestablished allocation figure would not.

Insitutional Setup

Because of the strong feeling among U.S. interests in 1979 that a sixteen-member Joint Fisheries Commission would usurp the newly acquired powers of the regional councils, the United States and Canada, in a future treaty, should consider a less politically stressful institutional arrangement. While an almost infinite variety of novel institutional arrangements might be hypothesized, from the very complex, such as a multifunctional, multimembered commission responsible for coordinating all ocean uses, to the very simple, such as a unifunctional, two-person commission responsible just for fisheries, the countries should consider working with the bureaucracies as they are in order to avoid bureaucratic paranoia and outcry over loss of regulatory powers.[19]

Two arrangements seem especially worthy of investigation. The first, a U.S. Regional Council-Canadian Regional Council arrangement, seems worthy because U.S. officials have on occasion raised the point with Canadian officials.[20] The second, a U.S. Oversight Committees-Canadian Working Groups arrangement, seems worthy because of its ready adaptability.

U.S. Regional Council-Canadian Council Institutional Arrangement: Handing joint management responsibilities over to regional councils in both countries has two positive attractions. It would be the ultimate in depoliticization on the U.S. side since the New England Council would remain in the forefront of planning. It would also ensure adequate representation to industry interests—fishermen and processors—since management would not be left in the hands of federal bureaucrats.

On the negative side, such an arrangement could be unwieldy since the combination of New England Council members (seventeen voting members, four nonvoting members) and Canadian counterparts could total forty-two members. The arrangement would also require major innovation by Canada, since a whole new regional council would have to be created, and perhaps cherished federal power would have to be delegated. Given industry's domination of the New England Council, serious doubts may also be raised concerning the ability of a council-council arrangement to make objective management decisions.

The dangers with a council-type arrangement have been noted by both government officials and academics. Giulio Pontecorvo has stated:

> [R]egional bodies which act to regulate an industry that is both directly and indirectly involved in international commerce may, by having different local needs and attitudes, create difficulties in establishing a consistent foreign policy ... No regional or local body, no matter how constructed or how constituted, is likely to move effectively and efficiently to enhance the general welfare. It seems clear, as Adam Smith so perceptively stated, that Councils composed of local producers will act in their own interest.[21]

Mr. Tony Campbell voiced his disapproval of a council-council suggestion in this way:

> They are something close to a disaster in terms of a unit with which you would negotiate. If you had two groups from either side all you would have is a collection of fairly raw interests with a very short

perspective and no real way of arriving at consensus. So from the point of view of delegating negotiating responsibilities at that level, I do not think it would work.[22]

Such negative judgments, however, should not preclude all consideration of such an arrangement. Perhaps the United States and Canada are caught in a difficult situation. If joint management is delegated to a regional council level, local interests might sabotage rational management. If joint management is elevated to an international commission level, local interests might sabotage the connective treaty bridge. Thus, the choice might never be between a good and an evil but between two evils. Neither must one be overly pessimistic about management at the council level. The New England Council has not left key groundfish—flounder, haddock, and cod—unmanaged. It has regulated Atlantic herring by tight quotas, and it has recently implemented a scallop management plan with a stringent control mechanism of forty meats per pound.

Council Oversight Committee-Canadian Working Groups Arrangement: Another option for institutional design would be to create not one council-council commission but to create six separate oversight committee-working group commissions.[23] The Demersal Finfish Oversight Committee of the New England Council and the Canadian Atlantic Groundfish Advisory Committee Working Group could coordinate groundfish management. The Council's Herring Oversight Committee and a Canadian Herring Work Group could coordinate herring management.[24] Other linkages could include a Scallop Oversight Committee with a Scallop Work Group, a Lobster Oversight Committee with a Scotia-Fundy Lobster Management Committee, a Mid-Atlantic Mackerel Oversight Committee with a Mackerel Work Group and a Mid-Atlantic Squid Oversight Committee with a Canadian Atlantic Groundfish Advisory Committee Working Group.

Such institutional matings promise at least four advantages. First, since the national institutions are almost all operational at present, very little conversion cost or effort would be required. Second, since joint management would be divided into six areas of expertise rather than an overall conglomerate, decisions might be easier and more informed. Third, memberships would be wieldy, with approximately ten to twenty members per oversight committee-work group. Fourth, Canada could retain federal control by limiting work-group membership to federal officials.

On the negative side, some council oversight committees might be dominated by industry interests, which could hinder rational management. The Canadian government, accustomed to more-central control over fisheries management than the United States, might hesitate to delegate much power to lower-echelon work groups.

Even so, perhaps the regional councils have ushered in a new era of regional control and power where national government to national government negotiations will no longer work. Regional oversight committees and regional work groups, close to regional interests, seem like the perfect land bases from which to work.

Dispute Settlement: The need for dispute settlement will depend on the extent of power delegated to the joint institution(s). If only recommendatory powers are granted, no dispute settlement would be necessary since no binding decisions would have to be made. If actual allocation and management decision making is delegated to the joint institution(s), some dispute-settlement procedure probably would be desired.

Since resort to third-party arbitration for dispute settlement was a major factor in the demise of the 1979 agreement, Canada and the United States should consider keeping dispute settlement between themselves in any future treaty. While numerous dispute-settlement procedures could be postulated, a procedure, borrowing from present national review mechanisms, seems most promising because of easy implementation and political acceptability.[25] In case of deadlock at the joint institution(s) level, review might simply proceed to joint consideration by the director general, Scotia Fundy Region, and the regional director, National Marine Fisheries Service, Northeast Region. For species having interregional implications for Canada, such as mackerel and pollock, review might alternatively proceed to the Atlantic Director Generals Committee and a corresponding U.S. group, headed by the regional director of the National Marine Fisheries Service. In case of deadlock at that level, the issue could proceed to joint consideration by the secretary of commerce and the minister of fisheries and oceans.

While lack of outside binding settlement could arguably induce both countries to avoid tough management decisions, the converse could just as well be true. That is, forcing officials into a "do or die" situation—resolving basic differences or reaching no binding joint-management decision—could facilitate management decisions. As one official has said: "[T]here is nothing that focuses the mind like the sure knowledge of being hanged in the morning."[26]

Executive Agreement

If the United States and Canada enter into a demonstrative agreement or a substantially modified administrative-distributive agreement, an executive-agreement form probably would be unnecessary and undesirable since the Senate would likely ratify a depoliticized treaty without incident. But if the two countries wish to enter a more politically stressful agreement—for example, one that expressly allocates fish stocks or one that establishes a binational commission—the executive-agreement form might become essential.

An executive agreement is an international commitment entered into by the executive departments of two or more states, usually by an exchange of letters. It is binding under international law, like a treaty, but in the case of the United States, it requires no Senate ratification.[27] The term *executive agreement* may broadly refer to any one of three situations: a presidential agreement authorized by a preexisting treaty, a presidential agreement authorized by congressional legislation or subsequently approved by Congress, and a presidential agreement made solely on the basis of the independent consitutional authority of the president. In a narrow sense, only the third situation, independent presidential commitments, would be termed executive agreements. The first two would be labeled international agreements other than treaties.

Concerning the feasibility of an executive agreement for joint fisheries mangement in the Gulf of Maine-Georges Bank region, two questions arise: When will U.S. law allow an executive agreement to circumvent the treaty form and Senate ratification? and Assuming the law does not forbid circumvention, when will U.S. diplomatic practice allow an executive agreement?

U.S. Law Concerning Executive Agreements

The Constitution, the Supreme Court, and Congress have articulated no clear line between an executive agreement and a treaty. The Constitution does not expressly mention executive agreements and contains only two brief references to treaty making.[28] Whatever executive-agreement-making powers the president enjoys must be inferred from rather nebulous constitutional sentences such as: "The executive power shall be vested in the President . . ."; "The President shall be Commander-in-Chief of the Army and Navy . . ."; "He shall . . . with the Advice and Consent of the Senate . . . appoint Ambassadors . . . and Consuls . . ."; and "He shall receive Ambassadors and other public Ministers; he shall take Care that the Laws be faithfully executed." When the Constitution does distinguish between "treaty" and "agreement or compact," it does not define such terms.[29]

The U.S. Supreme Court, meanwhile, has never directly ruled on a separation-of-powers challenge to Presidential executive-agreement-making power and thus has never etched a clear constitutional line between executive agreements and treaties.[30] The Court has, however, ruled on the legality of executive agreements and has spoken liberally of their need. In *United States* v. *Belmont*, the Court, in finding an executive agreement, which recognized the Soviet Union and assigned Soviet claims to the U.S. government, supreme to conflicting state law, stated:

The recognition, establishment of diplomatic relations, the assignment, and agreements with respect thereto, were all parts of one transaction, resulting in an international compact between the two governments. That the . . . agreements . . . were within the competence of the President may not be doubted. . . . [A]n international compact, as this was, is not always a treaty which requires the participation of the Senate. There are many such compacts, of which a protocol, a modus vivendi, a postal convention, and agreements like that now under consideration are illustrations.[31]

In a later case, upholding the same executive agreement, the Court again spoke favorably of the president's independent power to enter an executive agreement:

Power to remove such obstacles to full recognition as settlement of claims of our nationals certainly is a modest implied power of the President who is the "sole organ of the federal government in the field of international relations." Effectiveness in handling the delicate problems of foreign relations requires no less.[32]

Congress, while often discussing the need to trim the executive agreement-making power, has done little legislative clipping. The Case Act requires the secretary of state to forward all executive agreements to Congress "as soon as practicable" but no later than sixty days of entry into force.[33] The War Measures Act limits presidential deployment of armed forces to ninety days unless Congress declares war or approves the action.[34]

The scarcity of congressional legislation, of Supreme Court precedents, and of constitutional provisions concerning treaty making adds up to one surety. The legal door remains open for the United States and Canada to enter into an executive fisheries agreement for the Gulf of Maine-Georges Bank region.

U.S. Practice Concerning Executive Agreements

A survey of U.S. diplomatic practice regarding executive agreement making yields no clear line between executive agreements or treaties. Numerous major national commitments, such as the annexations of Texas and Hawaii and the entry into and carrying on the Korean and Vietnam wars, have surprisingly been implemented through executive agreements.[35] Many scholars have lamented the resultant impossibility of deciphering a pattern. For example, Professor Arthur Sutherland of Harvard Law School has stated:

They [executive agreements] have been used from the earliest days of independence of the United States; and thoughtful men have during all that time been unable to supply what the Constitution lacks— a clear distinction between what is appropriate matter for executive agreement, and what should be handled by treaty with Senatorial

concurrence. . . . We are as puzzled as President Monroe was in 1818 . . .
it is no more possible in our day than his to define one unknown in
terms of another.[36]

Three things are clear, however. First, the executive agreement has become a
favorite device. In 1930 the United States concluded 25 treaties to only 9 executive agreements. By 1968 the number of executive agreements leaped to 206
while the number of treaties fell to a mere 16.[37] As of January 1, 1972, the
United States was party to no fewer than 4,359 executive agreements to a
mere 947 treaties.[38] In the fisheries-management area, the United States has
entered into some 71 fisheries agreements between 1776 and 1979, with nearly
two-thirds being executive agreements.[39]

Second, the U.S. and Britain-Canada have often resorted to executive agreements to facilitate fisheries management. After the United States denounced the
1871 Treaty of Washington, an executive agreement allowed U.S. fishermen to
continue fishing in British waters, and vice versa, so as to avoid economic hard-
ships. In 1891 the United States and Britain entered an executive agreement
pledging a one-year moratorium on seal hunting to allow Bering Sea seal stocks
to replenish. During the early 1900s, while controversy brewed over U.S. fishing
rights off Newfoundland, a series of four executive agreements allowed U.S.
fishermen to continue purse seine fishing in exchange for Sunday observance
and customs obeyance.[40] From 1942 to 1957 Canada and the United States
cooperated in fur-seal conservation pursuant to executive agreements.[41] From
1970 to 1978, a series of executive agreements allowed Canadian fishermen
continued access to U.S. waters and vice versa in order to prevent economic
dislocations caused by extended jurisdictions.[42] More recently, the two countries have extended reciprocal tuna-fishing privileges by executive agreement.[43]

A third certainty is that current State Department guidelines for choosing
agreement types continue to allow wide official discretion. The eight factors
weighed in choosing agreement form follow:

1. Extent to which the agreement involves commitments or risks affecting
   the nation as a whole.
2. Whether the agreement is intended to affect state laws.
3. Whether the agreement can be given effect without the enactment of
   subsequent legislation by Congress.
4. Past U.S. practice as to similar agreements.
5. Preference of the Congress as to a particular type of agreement.
6. Degree of formality desired for an agreement.
7. Proposed duration of the agreement, the need for prompt conclusion of
   an agreement, and the desireability of concluding a routine or short-term
   agreement.
8. General international practice as to similar agreements.[44]

Given this wide official discretion, the numerous executive fisheries agreements in the past and a general U.S. favoritism toward streamlined diplomacy, an executive agreement covering fisheries management for the Gulf of Maine-Georges Bank certainly seems possible.

Informal Consultations

Instead of fisheries cooperation by treaty or executive agreement, the United States and Canada might enter no formal agreement and allow informal bridges of consultation to be deployed, as needed. Such an approach bears both negative and positive implications.

On the negative side, a lack of preordained consultations could induce apathetic bureaucrats to limit consultations to emergency situations. Myopic, short-term planning rather than strategic long-range planning could be the result. Also, lack of mandated joint decision making could result in much international talk but little cooperative action.

On the positive side, informal consultations avoid the vagaries of a two-thirds Senate vote. They avoid the creation of a whole new level of international bureaucracy. They are the ultimate in flexibility. And they allow national managers to travel familiar paths of consultation.

One should not underestimate the number of informal consultations currently occurring. Some tend to be well known, such as the yearly meetings between eastern Canadian premiers and eastern New England governors, the yearly discussions between American congressmen and Canadian parliamentarians through the Canada-U.S. Inter-Parliamentary Group, and the period meetings between the Canadian minister of fisheries and oceans and the U.S. secretary of commerce. Others tend to be less well known: the many formal meetings and workshops between Canadian and U.S. scientists over stock status and management,[45] the at-least-yearly consultations between the director general, Scotia-Fundy Region, and the regional director, National Marine Fisheries Service, Northeast Region.[46] A get-acquainted meeting took place in the late summer of 1981 in Lunenburg, Nova Scotia, between six members of the New England Council and Canadian officials.

Nor should one underestimate the practical effects of such meetings. For example, U.S. scientists assess Georges Bank herring, Gulf of Maine herring, and southwest Nova Scotia herring as one stock. Thus, the United States does consider Canadian harvests and does seek to coordinate its quota management at the scientific level.[47] Another example of joint management at the more-informal level occurred recently with scallops. When the New England Council's new scallop management plan threatened to hinder entry of Canadian scallop exports by requiring packaged scallops at the border to have no more than forty meats per pound, Canadian industry officials cried unfair trade restriction.[48] Canadian shipments, often packaged at fifty to sixty meats per pound because of restaurant requests or smaller scallop meats from the Bay of Fundy or Northumberland Strait, would have been effectively banned from U.S. entry. Informal consultations occurred at the international level and at the regional level between Alan Peterson, regional director, National Marine Fisheries Service, Northeast Region, and Richard Crouter, director general of the Scotia-Fundy Region. Finally, by an exchange of letters between Peterson and Crouter, the United States agreed to allow Canadian shipments with high meat counts in return for Canadian agreement to impose a forty meat count regulation on Canadian fishermen. All future Canadian scallop shipments will be certified by the Canadian government that the scallops therein were caught in accordance with the forty meat count regulation (which is the same as the U.S. regulation). It must be made clear that before the United States imposed a forty meat count on U.S. fishermen, Canada had in place a forty meat count on all scallops taken from the northeast peak of Georges for some time. What Canada was concerned with was the possession law which the United States was imposing along with its forty meat count legislation. The agreement that Crouter and Peterson worked out through the certification program was for the United States to allow scallops caught in Canadian waters under Canadian management programs to be authorized entry into the United States without having to meet its possession legislation. This meant that processors could continue to sort scallops to meet U.S. market demands and that those areas in which a forty meat count was not required by law (Bay of Fundy, Northumberland Strait) could export their scallops to the United States and not have to meet the U.S. possession legislation.[49]

Perhaps such successes mark the birth of a new era in joint fisheries management. No longer will lawyer-diplomats have to construct sophisticated, high-profile treaties or executive agreements. Fisheries managers will carry on their consultations as needed.

Notes

1. Such a result would probably be most likely if the United States wins all of Georges Bank, since stock overlap, and thus the need for joint management, would then be minimal. Such a result may also be read in UNCLOS III. The negative vote by the United States perhaps indicates a free-enterprise, do-it-myself attitude, representative of the Reagan administration, which could extend to other areas of U.S. policy such as fisheries. The free-enterprise attitude may already be reflected in present U.S. management of Atlantic groundfish where only minimal management restrictions, such as mesh size and fish size, are in place.

2. For example, the allocation percentages might be varied to account for the geographical configuration of the boundary line and the categories might be changed from three to two: A stocks (transboundary/joint management) and B stocks (stationary/consultative management).

3. There is, of course, no similar situation under the Canadian constitutional system where the federal cabinet, through the governor-general, ratifies international agreements and only seeks parliamentary approval as a matter of discretionary practice. *See* A. Gotlieb, *Canadian Treaty-Making* 13-19 (1968).

4. For a history of the various conflicts involving numerous vessel seizures and numerous treaty abrogations, *see* D. Johnston, *The International Law of Fisheries* 190-202 (1965), and F. Redding, *Sharing the Living Resources of the Sea: An Analysis of Contemporary American-Canadian Fisheries Relations* 30-39 (Ph.D. Thesis, University of Oklahoma, 1979).

5. R. Dangerfield, *In Defense of the Senate* 244 (1933).

6. H. Keenleyside, *Canada and the United States* 271-272 (1929).

7. Dangerfield, *supra* note 5, at 244.

8. *Id.*

9. W. Willoughby, *The Joint Organizations of Canada and the United States* 73-74 (1979).

10. Canada refused ratification for two reasons. First, the Senate amendment, by seeking extension to all British nationals, insulted Canada's sense of national pride. Second, the amendment would have required Canada to undertake the impossible task of submitting the treaty for ratification to all parliaments in the British Empire. Dangerfield, *supra* note 5, at 208-210.

11. Minutes of the House of Commons Standing Committee on Fisheries and Forestry, 32d Parliament, 1st sess., Issue No. 13, at 16-17 (October 14, 1980).

12. Minutes of the House of Commons Standing Committee on Fisheries and Forestry, 32d Parliament, 1st sess., Issue No. 35, at 25 (May 29, 1981).

13. External Affairs Canada, *Statements and Speeches* No. 80/22 (Address to the Eleventh Leadership Conference of the Centre for the Study of the Presidency, Ottawa, Ontario, October 18, 1980).

14. Demonstrative, administrative, and distributive treaties are three of the four major types of international agreement. The fourth type, a resolutive agreement—designed to resolve an outstanding issue such as the Gulf of Maine boundary dispute—could also be used in case of future, specific, fisheries emergencies between the two countries. Since emergencies are what joint management would seek to avoid, however, further discussion of the resolutive-type agreement is beyond the scope of this book. For a general discussion of the four types of international agreement, *see* D. Johnston and L. Enomoto, "Regional Approaches to the Protection and Conservation of the Marine Environment," *in* D. Johnston (ed.); *The Environmental Law of the Sea* 356-357 (1981); and D. Johnston, *Environmental Management in the South China Sea: Legal and Institutional*

Developments, East-West Environment and Policy Institute, Research Report No. 10 at 69–71 (May 1982).

15. That equity should be the legal touchstone for allocating transboundary fisheries draws support from at least four sources. First, analogy may be drawn to continental-shelf boundary-delimitation cases that have invoked the concept of equitable principles. *See* North Sea Continental Shelf Cases (*Federal Republic of Germany* v. *Denmark; Federal Republic of Germany* v. *Netherlands*), [1969] I.C.J. 3, 49–53 and Anglo-French Arbitration (*United Kingdom* v. *France*), 18 Int'l Legal Materials 397–420. Second, analogy might be drawn to the fisheries jurisdiction cases that invoked the principle of equitable sharing. *See* Fisheries Jurisdiction Cases (*United Kingdom* v. *Iceland; Federal Republic of Germany* v. *Iceland*), [1974] I.C.J. 3, 175, *reprinted in* 13 Int'l Legal Materials 1049, 1090 (Rights to Fishing in Iceland's 50-mile Exclusive Fishing Zone). Third, reference might be made to the law of the sea treaty's reliance on "equitable solution" for delimiting opposite or adjacent continental shelves and exclusive economic zones. *See* Draft Convention on the Law of the Sea, arts. 74 (Economic Zone) and 83 (Continental Shelf), U.N. Doc. A/CONF. 62/L.78 (August 28, 1981). Fourth, reference may be made to a recent U.N. Resolution entitled, "Co-operation in the Field of the Environment Concerning Natural Resources Shared by Two or More States," which recommends "equitable utilization" as a guiding principle in resource allocations. *See* U.N. Doc. A/- 34/186 (December 18, 1979), *which incorporates the fifteen guiding principles in* the Report of the Intergovernmental Working Group of Experts on Natural Resources Shared by Two or More States on the Work of Its Fifth Session Held at Nairobi from January 23, to February 7, 1978, UNEP GC .6/17; *reprinted in* 17 Int'l Legal Materials 1094–99. For a general overview of the evolving nature of equity in international law, *see* Collins and Rogoff, *The International Law of Maritime Boundary Delimitation* 34 Me. L. Rev. 1 (1982).

16. *See e.g.,* B. Rothschild (ed.), *World Fisheries Policy Multidisciplinary Views* 111 (1972); S. Oda, *International Control of Sea Resources* 230 (1962); H. Knight (ed.), *The Future of International Fisheries Management* 27-37 (1975); H. Knight, *The Law of the Sea: Cases, Documents, and Readings* 667-68 (1975-1976); and F. T. Christy, "Distribution Systems for World Fisheries: Problems and Principles," *in Perspectives on Ocean Policy* (Conference on Ocean Relations in Airlie, Virginia, October 21-24, 1974).

17. Minutes of the House of Commons Standing Committee on Fisheries and Forestry, 32d Parliament, 1st sess., Issue No. 35, at 26 (May 29, 1981).

18. Delegation could be express or implied. The treaty might expressly provide: "the Institution shall seek to apportion the catch of each stock between the two nations, according to the following principles: A, B, C, D . . . " Or the treaty might be silent concerning allocation which would, then, leave allocation within institutional discretion.

19. For a general discussion of possible binational arrangements, *see* K. Beauchamp, *The Management Function of Ocean Boundaries: Prospects for Cooperative Ocean Management between Canada and the United States* 270–280 (LL.M. Thesis, Dalhousie Law School, 1981).

20. *See* Senate Debates, 32d Parliament, 1st sess., Volume 128, No. 38, at 670 (July 15, 1980).

21. G. Pontecorvo, *Fishery Management and the General Welfare: Implications of the New Structure,* 52 Wash. L. Rev. 641, 654 (1977).

22. Minutes of the House of Commons Standing Committee on Fisheries and Forestry, 32d Parliament, 1st sess., Issue No. 13, at 37 (October 14, 1980) (Statement of Mr. Tony Campbell, Director General, International Directorate, Department of Fisheries and Oceans.

23. Although six intitutional arrangements are suggested since they would encompass all fifteen fish species covered by the 1979 agreement, not all six may be necessary in practice. Scallops and lobster, because of nonmigratory behavior, might not need joint management. Squid and mackerel, because of underutilization, might not require joint management for at least the near future.

24. The S.W. Nova Scotia Work Group might be impressed into service, or if desired by the Department of Fisheries and Oceans, a smaller, all-federal work group might be established for international purposes.

For herring within state territorial waters, an additional "Commission" might be established, consisting of a State Committee headed by Maine's Commissioner of Marine Resources and a Canadian Work Group headed by the Area Manager in St. Andrews, New Brunswick.

25. For a general discussion of dispute settlement between the United States and Canada, *see* Joint Proceedings, Canadian Council on International Law, 6th Annual Conference and Canada-United States Law Institute, 1st Annual Conference, *Canada-U.S. Relations: Co-operation and Dispute Settlement in the North American Context,* 1 Canada–United States L.J. 1–169 (Summer, 1978). For a summary of the law of the sea treaty's procedures for dispute settlement concerning living resources, *see* C. de Klemm, "Living Resources of the Ocean," *in* D. Johnston (ed.), *The Environmental Law of the Sea* 146–147 (1981).

26. Minutes of the House of Commons Standing Committee on Fisheries and Forestry, 32d Parliament, 1st sess., Issue No. 35, at 14 (May 29, 1981) (Statement of Mr. Legault).

27. That treaties and executive agreements are equally binding under international law is supported by at least three foundations. The 1969 Vienna Convention on the Law of Treaties draws no distinction between treaties and executive agreements. *See* U.N. Conference on the Law of Treaties, art. 2, Doc. A/CONF. 39/27, May 23, 1969. The International Court of Justice has treated the agreements as interchangeable. *See e.g.,* Fisheries Jurisdiction Case (*Federal*

Republic of Germany v. *Iceland*), 1974 I.C.J. 175, 193, *reprinted in* 13 Int'l Legal Materials 1090, 1099 (1974). Numerous scholars have argued for interchangeability. *See, e.g.,* McDougal and Lans, *Treaties and Congressional-Executive or Presidential Agreements: Interchangeable Instruments of National Policy: I* 54 Yale L.J. 181, 318–331 (1945).

For arguments that executive agreements do not have the same binding effect under international law (for example, executive agreements only bind the signing executive and are terminable at will), *see* Borchard, *Treaties and Executive Agreements—A Reply* 54 Yale L.J. 616 (1945).

28. Article 1, Section 10, provides: "No State shall enter into any Treaty, Alliance, or Confederation. . . . No State shall, without the Consent of Congress . . . enter into any Agreement or Compact with another State, or with a foreign Power." Article II, Section 2 provides: "The President . . . shall have power, by and with the Advice and Consent of the Senate, to make Treaties, provided two thirds of the Senators present concur."

29. U.S. Const. art. II, § 1, cl. 1; U.S. Const. art. II, § 2, cl. 1; U.S. Const. art. II, § 2, cl. 2; U.S. Const. art. II, § 3; U.S. Const. art. I, § 10.

30. For a lower federal decision ruling on such a challenge, *see Dole* v. *Carter,* 444 F. Supp. 1065 (D.C. Kansas 1977). There the court upheld President Carter's executive agreement returning Hungarian coronation regalia to Hungary against Senator Robert Dole's charge of senate treaty-making usurpation.

31. 301 U.S. 324, 330–331 (1937).

32. *United States* v. *Pink,* 315 U.S. 203, 229 (1942). For earlier Supreme Court decisions not ruling on the validity of executive agreements but referring positively to the president's executive power, *see Altman & Co.* v. *United States,* 224 U.S. 583 (1912) and *United States* v. *Curtiss-Wright Corp.* 299 U.S. 304 (1936). For a lower federal decision invalidating an executive agreement as beyond presidential power, *see Marschalk Co., Inc.* v. *Iran Nat. Airlines Corp.,* 518 F. Supp. 69 (S.D.N.Y. 1981) (president's agreement to terminate all legal proceedings in the United States against Iran in exchange for U.S. hostages violated the separation of powers doctrine and the Fifth Amendment). But see *American International Group* v. *Islamic Republic of Iran,* 657 F.2d 430 (D.C. Cir. 1981) and *Dames & Moore* v. *Regan,* 101 5 Ct. 2972 (1981) (president's executive agreement with Iran upheld against constitutional attack).

33. 1 U.S.C.A. § 112(b) (Supp. 1982). In case of security precautions, the agreement would be referred to the Senate Foreign Relations Committee and the House Committee on International Relations.

34. 50 U.S.C.A. § 1541, 1544 (Supp. 1982).

35. The Texas and Hawaii agreements were first defeated as treaties by the U.S. Senate. Later both houses of Congress approved the executive agreements by Joint Resolution. J. Paige, *The Law Nobody Knows* 47–55 (1977).

For a review of executive agreement making as to Korea and Vietnam, *see* A. Gilbert, *Executive Agreements and Treaties, 1946–1973* (1973).

36. Sutherland, *Restricting the Treaty Power* 65 Harv. L. Rev. 1305, 1324 (1952), *quoted in* Hearings on Senate Resolution No. 486, Before the Committee on Foreign Relations United States Senate, 94th Cong., 2d Sess. at 97 (July 21, 28, 1976).

37. M. Whiteman, *Digest of International Law* Vol. 14, p. 210 (1970).

38. R. Stebbins and E. Adam, *American Foreign Relations 1972* 21 (1976).

39. Such a figure should be treated as approximate for three reasons. First, such a figure is based on public records such as the U.S. Treaties Series. Not all executive agreements, particularly lower-echelon departmental agreements, necessarily appear in such records. Second, the figure includes a number of treaties having fisheries provisions, which others might label peace treaties or commerce treaties (such as the 1783 Treaty of Peace). Third, the figure only includes parent agreements, not every amendment or change. For example, the six individual executive agreements covering Polish fishing in the western mid-Atlantic from 1969 to 1976 are treated as one. *See* 20 U.S.T. 884 T.I.A.S. No. 6704; 21 U.S.T. 1335 T.I.A.S. No. 6890; 22 U.S.T. 2190 T.I.A.S. No. 7264; 23 U.S.T. 1254 T.I.A.S. No. 7397; 24 U.S.T. 1519 T.I.A.S. No. 7659; 26 U.S.T. 1117 T.I.A.S. 8099.

40. 1 Malloy 729, 743, 805–808, 811, 832, 844. For a general discussion of the executive agreements, *see* W. McClure, *International Executive Agreements* 77–78 (1967).

41. 6 Bevans 297 (1942), 6 Bevans 457 (1947), 3 U.S.T. 3896 T.I.A.S. No. 2521 (1952). Canada and the United States entered into a North Pacific Fur Seals Convention in 1957 with the Soviet Union and Japan. 8 U.S.T. 2283, T.I.A.S. No. 3948.

42. 21 U.S.T. 1283 T.I.A.S. No. 6879; 23 U.S.T. 622 T.I.A.S. No. 7323; 24 U.S.T. 1729 T.I.A.S. No. 7676; 24 U.S.T. 959 T.I.A.S. No. 7606; 25 U.S.T. 653 T.I.A.S. No. 7818; 26 U.S.T. 554 T.I.A.S. No. 8052; 27 U.S.T. 1365 T.I.A.S. No. 8251; 28 U.S.T. 5571 T.I.A.S. No. 8648.

43. August 21, 1980 T.I.A.S. No. 10024.

44. 11 Foreign Affairs Manual 721.3 (July 12, 1976).

45. A government report lists binational meetings between scientists for herring, groundfish, and lobster. *See* Department of Fisheries and Oceans, *Canadian Atlantic Fisheries Scientific Advisory Committee (CAFSAC) Annual Report 1977–1978 Volume 1* 21, 25, 36 (1978).

46. Personal interview, Richard Crouter, director-general, Scotia-Fundy Region, Department of Fisheries and Oceans (July 20, 1982).

47. *See* New England Fishery Management Council, *Amendment No. 3 to the Fishery Management Plan for the Atlantic Herring Fishery of the Northwest Atlantic*, 45 Fed. Reg. 15957 (March 12, 1980).

48. *See, e.g.,* Halifax Chronicle-Herald, January 25, 1982, at 1-2, and Halifax Chronicle Herald, March 11, 1982, at 4.

49. Personal interview, Richard Crouter, director-general, Scotia-Fundy Region, Department of Fisheries and Oceans (July 20, 1982).

Appendix A: Model Demonstrative Treaty

The key provisions of a demonstrative treaty might read as follows:

The government of the United States of America and the Government of Canada,

Considering their common concern for the rational management, conservation, and optimum utilization of fish stocks off the east coast;

Considering stocks A, B, C, D . . . are transboundary in nature;

Considering the possibility for fishing by one country to negatively affect the fishing in the other;

Considering the need to harmonize fishing efforts, according to the principle of equitable utilization, giving due regard to geographic distribution of fish stocks, to historical patterns of fishing, and to the social, economic, and environmental needs of both countries;

Hereby agree as follows:

1. To the extent possible, common fish stocks should be managed as a unit;

2. To facilitate coordination of national management regimes, all informal consultations between the two countries should continue;

3. To further coordination, the relevant Council Oversight Committees and the relevant Canadian Work Groups, for each transboundary stock, should consult at least once a year to discuss promulgated or proposed fishing plans;

4. To facilitate communication, Canada should send a representative or representatives to major meetings of the New England and Mid-Atlantic Councils dealing with transboundary stocks, and the United States should send a representative or representatives to major meetings of Canadian Advisory Committees dealing with transboundary stocks.

5. To evaluate the implementation of this Agreement, to consider deletions or additions to the list of transboundary stocks, and to discuss the need for more formal arrangements, the two governments shall consult on a yearly basis.

Appendix B: Statutes

Canada

Arctic Waters Pollution Prevention Act, R.S.C. 1970 (1st Supp.) C. 2.

Coastal Fisheries Protection Act, R.S.C. 1970, C. C-21.

Department of Fisheries Act, S.C. 1930, C. 21.

Fisheries Act, R.S.C. 1970, C. F-14.

Fisheries Development Act, R.S.C. 1970, C. F-21.

Fisheries Improvement Loans Act, R.S.C. 1970, C. F-22.

Fisheries Price Support Act, R.S.C. 1970, C. F-23.

Fishery and Recreational Harbours Act, S.C. 1977–1978, C. 30.

Fish Inspection Act, R.S.C. 1970, C. F-12.

Government Organization Act 1969, S.C. 1968-1969, C. 28.

Government Organization Act 1970, S.C. 1970-1971-1972, Vol. 1, C. 42.

Government Organization Act 1979, S.C. 1978-1979, C. 13.

The Saltfish Act, R.S.C. 1970 (1st Supp.), C. 37.

Territorial Sea and Fishing Zones Act, S.C. 1964, C. 22.

Unemployment Insurance Act, R.S.C. 1970, C. U-2.

United States

American Fisheries Promotion Act of 1980, Pub. L. 96-561, tit. 2, 94 Stat. 3296.

Bartlett Act, 16 U.S.C.A. §§ 1091–1094 (1974).

Case Act, 1 U.S.C.A. § 112(b) (Supp. 1982).

Enrollment of Vessels Act, 46 U.S.C.A. § 252 et seq. (1958).

Home Port Act, 46 U.S.C.A. § 1011 et seq. (1976).

Federal Advisory Committee Act, 5 U.S.C. App. §§ 1-15 (1976).

Fishery Conservation and Management Act, 16 U.S.C.A. §§ 1801–1882 (Supp. 1980).

National Environmental Policy Act, 42 U.S.C.A. § § 4321–4361 (1976).

Outer Continental Shelf Lands Act of 1953, 43 U.S.C.A. § § 1331–1343 (1964).

Ship Registry and Recording Law, 46 U.S.C.A. § 11 et seq.

Submerged Lands Act, 43 U.S.C.A. § § 1301–1315 (1974).

War Measures Act, 50 U.S.C.A. § § 1541–1548 (Supp. 1982).

Appendix C: Cases

Canada

Supreme Court

Attorney-General for British Columbia v. *Attorney-General for Canada (British Columbia Fisheries Reference),* (1914) A.C. 153, 15 D.L.R. 308 (P.C. 1913).

Attorney-General for Canada v. *Attorney-General for British Columbia (Fish Canneries),* (1930) A.C. 111, (1929) 3 W.W.R. 449, (1930) 1 D.L.R. 194 (P.C. 1929).

Attorney-General for Canada v. *Attorney-General for Ontario, Quebec and Nova Scotia (The Fisheries Case),* (1898) A.C. 700 (P.C.).

Attorney General for Canada v. *Attorney-General for Quebec (Quebec Fisheries),* (1921) 1 A.C. 413, 56 D.L.R. 358 (P.C. 1920).

Fowler v. *The Queen,* (1980) 32 N.R. 230.

Northwest Falling Contractors Ltd. v. *The Queen,* (1980) 32 N.R. 541, 2 S.C.R. 292.

The Queen v. *Robertson,* (1882) 6 S.C.R. 52.

In re Provincial Fisheries, (1895) 26 S.C.R. 444.

Reference re Ownership of Offshore Mineral Rights, (1967) S.C.R. 792, 65 D.L.R. 2d 353.

Provincial Court

Attorney-General of Canada v. *Aluminum Co. of Canada Ltd.,* (1980) 115 D.L.R. 3d 495.

The Queen v. *Forest Protection Ltd.,* (1978) 20 N.B.R. 2d 653, 34 A.P.R. 653, 7 C.E.L.R. 93.

United States

Altman & Co. v. *United States,* 224 U.S. 583 (1912).

Bayside Fish Co. v. *Gentry,* 297 U.S. 422 (1936).

California v. *Zook,* 336 U.S. 725 (1944).

Cooley v. *Board of Wardens,* 53 U.S. (12 How.) 299 (1851).

Douglas v. *Seacoast Products, Inc.,* 431 U.S. 265 (1977).

Exxon Corp. v. *Governor of Md.,* 437 U.S. 117 (1978).

Foster Packing Co. v. *Haydel,* 278 U.S. 1 (1928).

Hughes v. *Oklahoma,* 441 U.S. 322 (1979).

Louisiana v. *Mississippi,* 202 U.S. 1 (1905).

Manchester v. *Massachusetts,* 139 U.S. 240 (1890).

McCready v. *Virginia,* 94 U.S. 391 (1876).

Missouri v. *Holland,* 252 U.S. 416 (1920).

Skiriotes v. *Florida,* 313 U.S. 69 (1941).

Toomer v. *Witsell,* 334 U.S. 385 (1948).

Tukahashi v. *Fish and Game Commission,* 334 U.S. 410 (1948).

United States v. *Belmont,* 301 U.S. 324 (1937).

United States v. *California,* 332 U.S. 19 (1947).

United States v. *Curtiss-Wright Export Corp.,* 299 U.S. 304 (1936).

United States v. *Florida et al.,* 363 U.S. 121 (1960).

United States v. *Louisiana,* 339 U.S. 699 (1950).

United States v. *Louisiana et al.,* 363 U.S. 1 (1960).

United States v. *Maine,* 420 U.S. 515 (1978).

United States v. *Pink,* 315 U.S. 203 (1942).

United States v. *Texas,* 339 U.S. 707 (1950).

Federal

American International Group v. *Islamic Republic of Iran,* 657 F.2d 430 (D.C. Cir. 1981).

Dole v. *Carter,* 444 F. Supp. 1065 (D.C. Kansas 1977).

Felton v. *Hodges,* 374 F.2d 337 (5th Cir. 1967).

Marschalk Co., Inc. v. *Iran Nat. Airlines Corp.,* 518 F. Supp. 69 (S.D.N.Y. 1981).

Treasure Salvors v. *Unidentified Wreck, Etc.* . 569 F.2d 330 (5th Cir. 1978).

State

California v. *Weeren*, 607 P.2d 1279 (1980).

Employers Mutual Casualty Co. v. *Samuels*, 407 S.W. 2d 839 (Tex. Civ. App. 1966).

People v. *Foretich*, 14 Cal. App. 3d 6, 92 Cal. Rptr. 481 (1970).

State v. *Bundrant*, 546 P.2d 530 (Alaska 1976).

International

Anglo-French Arbitration (United Kingdom v. *France)*, 18 Int'l Legal Materials 397.

Fisheries Jurisdiction Cases (United Kingdom v. *Iceland; Federal Republic of Germany* v. *Iceland)*, (1974) I.C.J. 3, 175.

North Sea Continental Shelf Cases (Federal Republic of Germany v. *Denmark; Federal Republic of Germany* v. *Netherlands)* (1969) I.C.J. 3.

Bibliography

Books

Apollonio, Spencer. *The Gulf of Maine.* Rockland, Me.: Courier-Gazette, 1979.

Daborn, G.R., ed. *Fundy Tidal Power and the Environment.* Wolfville, Nova Scotia: Acadia University Institute, 1977.

Dangerfield, Royden J. *In Defense of the Senate.* Port Washington, N.Y.: Kennikat Press, 1966.

Fleming, Denna Frank. *The Treaty Veto of the American Senate.* New York: G.P. Putnam's Sons, 1930.

Gilbert, Amy M. *Executive Agreements and Treaties, 1946-1973.* Endicott, N.Y. Thomas-Newall, 1973.

Gotlieb, A.E., *Canadian Treaty-Making.* Toronto: Butterworths, 1968.

Gusey, W. *The Fish and Wildlife Resources of the Georges Bank Region.* Houston: Shell Oil Company, 1977.

Hogg, Peter W. *Constitutional Law of Canada.* Toronto: Carswell Co., 1977.

Hollick, Ann L. *U.S. Foreign Policy and the Law of the Sea.* Princeton, N.J.: Princeton University Press, 1981.

Holt, W. Stull. *Treaties Defeated by the Senate.* Baltimore: John Hopkins Press, 1933.

Johnson, Barbara, and Zacher, Mark W. *Canadian Foreign Policy and the Law of the Sea.* Vancouver: University of British Columbia Press, 1977.

Johnston, Douglas M. *The International Law of Fisheries.* New Haven: Yale University Press, 1965.

————, ed. *The Environmental Law of the Sea.* Gland, Switzerland: International Union for Conservation of Nature and Natural Resources, 1981.

Juda, Lawrence. *Ocean Space Rights: Developing U.S. Policy.* New York: Praeger Publishers, 1975.

Keenleyside, Hugh L. *Canada and the United States.* Port Washington, N.Y.: Kennikat Press, 1971.

Knight, H. Gary. *The Law of the Sea: Cases, Documents, and Readings.* Washington, D.C.: Nautilus Press, 1975.

————, ed. *The Future of International Fisheries Management.* St. Paul, Minn.: West Publishing Co., 1975.

LaForest, Gerard V. *Natural Resources and Public Property under the Canadian Constitution.* Toronto: University of Toronto Press, 1969.

Laevastu, T., and Larkins, H. *Marine Fisheries Ecosystem: Its Quantititive Evaluation and Management.* Surrey, England: Fishing News Books, 1981.

Landberg, L.A. *Bibliography for the Anthropological Study of Fishing Industries and Maritime Communities.* Kingston, R.I.: University of Rhode Island, Center for Marine Resource Development, 1979.

Leim, A.H., and Scott, W.B. *Fishes of the Atlantic Coast of Canada.* Ottawa Queen's Printer, 1966.

Lorimer, Rowland and Stanley E. McMullin, eds. *Canada and the Sea.* Willowdale, Ontario: The Association for Canadian Studies, 1980.

McClure, Wallace. *International Executive Agreements.* New York: AMS Press, 1967.

McConnell, W.H. *Commentary on the British North America Act.* Toronto Macmillan, 1977.

Macdonald, R.St.J., Morris, G.L.; and Johnston, D.M., eds. *Canadian Perspectives on International Law and Organization.* Toronto: University of Toronto Press, 1974.

McLeod, G., and Prescott, J., eds. *Georges Bank—Past, Present and Future of a Marine Environment.* Boulder, Colo.: Westview Press, 1982.

Malloy, William M. *Treaties, Conventions, International Acts, Protocols and Agreements Between the United States of America and Other Powers 1776-1937.* Washington D.C.: Government Printing Office, 1910.

Maritime Ocean Resources Ltd. *The Canadian Fisheries and Ocean Industries Directory.* Halifax, Nova Scotia: Maritime Ocean Resources, 1981.

Oda, S. *International Control of Sea Resources.* Leyden: A.W. Sijthoff, 1963.

Paige, Joseph. *The Law Nobody Knows.* New York: Vantage Press, 1977.

Pontecorvo, G., ed. *Fisheries Conflicts in the North Atlantic: Problems of Management and Jurisdiction.* Cambridge, Mass.: Ballinger Publishing, 1974.

Rhode Island University. Center for Ocean Management Studies. *Comparative Marine Policy: Perspectives from Europe, Scandinavia, Canada and the United States.* New York: Praeger Publishers, 1981.

Rothschild, Brian J., ed. *World Fisheries Policy Multidisciplinary Views.* Seattle: University of Washington Press, 1972.

Stebbins, Richard P., and Adam, Elaine P. *American Foreign Relations 1972: A Documentary Record.* New York: New York University Press, 1976.

Tribe, Lawrence H. *American Constitutional Law.* Mineola, N.Y.: Foundation Press, 1978.

Whiteman, Marjorie M. *Digest of International Law.* Washington, D.C.: U.S. Government Printing Office, 1970.

Wiktor, Christian L., and Tanguay, G. *Constitutions of Canada: Federal and Provincial.* Dobbs Ferry, N.Y.: Oceana Publications, 1978.

Willoughby, William R. *The Joint Organizations of Canada and the United States.* Toronto: University of Toronto Press, 1979.

Journals

Anson and Schenkkan. *Federalism, the Dormant Commerce Clause, and State-Owned Resources.* 59 Tex. L. Rev. 71 (1980).

Bigelow and Schroeder. *Fishes of the Gulf of Maine.* 53 U.S. Fish & Wildlife Serv. Bull. 1-577 (1953).

Brochard. *Treaties and Executive Agreements–A Reply.* 54 Yale L.J. 616 (1945).

Boyer et al. *Seasonal Distribution and Growth of Larval Herring (Clupea Harengus L.) in the Georges Bank-Gulf of Maine Area from 1962 to 1970.* 35(1) J. Int'l Council Explor. Sea 36-51 (June 1973).

Coggins. *Wildlife and the Constitution: The Walls Come Tumbling Down.* 55 Wash. L. Rev. 295 (1980).

Collins and Rogoff. *The International Law of Maritime Boundary Delimitation.* 34 Me. L. Rev. 1 (1982).

Colton. *The Enigma of Georges Bank Spawning.* 6 Limnology and Oceanography 280 (1961).

Comment. *Boundary Delimitation in the Economic Zone: The Gulf of Maine Dispute.* 30 Me. L. Rev. 207 (1979).

Comment. *Constitutionality of State Fishery Zones in the High Seas: The Oregon Fisheries Conservation Zone Act.* 55 Or. L. Rev. 141 (1976).

Comment. *The Fishery Conservation and Management Act of 1976: State Regulations under the Fishery Conservation and Management Act of 1976.* 52 Wash. L. Rev. 599 (1977).

Donaldson and Pontecorvo. *Economic Rationalization of Fisheries: The Problem of Conflicting National Interests on Georges Bank.* 8 Ocean Devel. and Int'l L.J. 149 (1980).

Fairley. *Canadian Federalism, Fisheries and the Constitution: External Constraints on Internal Ordering.* 12 Ottawa L. Rev. 257 (1980).

Greene. *Domestic Factors and Canada-United States Fisheries Relations.* 13(4) J. Political Science 731-750 (December 1980).

Gulland. *The Concept of the Marginal Yield from Exploited Fish Stocks.* 32 J. Cons. Per. Int'l Explor. Mer. 256-261 (1968).

Gulland and Boerema. *Scientific Advice on Catch Levels.* 71 Fishery Bulletin 325-335 (1973).

Harrison. *Jurisdiction over the Canadian Offshore: A Sea of Confusion.* 17 Osgoode L. J. 469 (1979).

Harrison. *The Offshore Mineral Resources Agreement in the Maritime Provinces.* 4 Dalhousie L.J. 245 (1978).

Iles and Sinclair. *Atlantic Herring Stock Discreteness and Abundance.* 215 Science 627 (February 5, 1982).

Jacobson and Cameron. *Potential Conflicts between a Future Law of the Sea Treaty and the Fishery Conservation and Management Act of 1976.* 52 Wash. L. Rev. 451 (1977).

Johnston. *Legal and Diplomatic Developments in the Northwest Atlantic Fisheries.* 4 Dalhousie L.J. 37 (1977).

Joint Proceedings. Canadian Council on International Law. 6th Annual Conference and Canada-United States Law Institute, 1st Annual Conference.

Canada-U.S. Relations: Co-operation and Dispute Settlement in the North American Context. 1 Canada-Untied States L.J. 1–169 (Summer, 1978).

LaForest. *Canadian Inland Waters of the Atlantic Provinces and the Bay of Fundy Incident.* 1 Can. Yearbook Int. L. 149 (1963).

Levitan. *The Foreign Relations Power.* 54 Yale L.J. 467 (1946).

McDougal and Lans. *Treaties and Congressional-Executive or Presidential Agreements: Interchangeable Instruments of National Policy.* 59 Yale L.J. 181 (1945).

Murphy. *Treaties and International Agreements Other Than Treaties: Constitutional Allocation of Power and Responsibility among President, the House of Representatives and the Senate.* 23 Kan. L. Rev. 221 (1975).

Note. *Congressional Authorization and Oversight of International Fishery Agreements Under the Fishery Conservation and Management Act of 1976.* 52 Wash. L. Rev. 495 (1977).

Note. *Law of the Sea: Protection of United States Fishing Interests—American Fisheries Promotion Act of 1980.* 22 Harv. Int'l L.J. 485 (1981).

Note. *Territorial Jurisdiction—Massachusetts Judicial Extension Act—State Legislature Extends Jurisdiction of State Court to 200 Miles at Sea.* 5 Vand. J. Transnat'l L. 490 (1972).

Perry. *Principle of Equal Protection.* 32 Hastings L.J. 1133 (1981).

Pontecorvo. *Fishery Management and the General Welfare: Implications of the New Structure.* 52 Wash. L. Rev. 641 (1977).

Posgay. *Movement of Tagged Sea Scallops on Georges Bank.* 43(4) Marine Fisheries Review 19–25 (April 1981).

Rhee. *The Application of Equitable Principles to Resolve the United States-Canada Dispute Over East Coast Fishery Resources.* 21 Harv. Int'l L.J. 667 (1980).

————.*Equitable Solutions to the Maritime Boundary Dispute between the United States and Canada in the Gulf of Maine.* 75 Am. J. Int'l L. 590 (1980).

Rogalski. *The Unique Federalism of the Regional Councils under the Fishery Conservation and Management Act of 1976.* 9 B.C. Env. Aff. L. Rev. 163 (1980).

Schoenbaum and McDonald. *State Management of Marine Fisheries after the Fishery Conservation and Management Act of 1976 and Douglas V. Seacoast Products, Inc.* 19 Wm. & Mary L. Rev. 17 (1977-1978).

Sette. *Biology of the Atlantic Mackerel of North America, Part II: Migrations and Habits.* 51 U.S. Fish & Wildlife Serv. Bull. 251–315 (1950).

Snow. *Extended Fishery Jurisdiction in Canada and the United States.* 5 Ocean Devel. and Int'l L.J. 291 (1978).

Sutherland. *Restricting the Treaty Power.* 65 Harv. L. Rev. 1305 (1952).

Varat. *"State Citizenship" and Interstate Equality.* 48 Chi. L. Rev. 487 (1981).

Wang. *Canada-United States Fisheries and Maritime Boundary Negotiations: Diplomacy in Deep Water.* 38/39 Behind the Headlines 1 (1981).

Papers and Reports

Anderson, E.D.; Lax, F.E.; and Almizida, E.P. "The Silver Hake Stocks and Fishery Off Northeastern United States." National Marine Fisheries Service, Northeast Fisheries Center, Woods Hole Laboratory, Lab. Ref. No. 79-28, July 10, 1979.

Anderson, E.D., and Overholtz, W.J. "Status of the Northwest Atlantic Mackerel Stock-1979." National Marine Fisheries Service, Northeast Fisheries Center, Woods Hole Laboratory, Lab. Ref. No. 79-35, August 1979.

Bolivar, David. "Canada/United States East Coast Fisheries Treaty—An Over-View." Paper presented to the Halifax Branch of the Canadian Institute of International Affairs, January 22, 1981.

Brown, B. "The Status of the Fishery Resources on Georges Bank." National Marine Fisheries Service, Northeast Fisheries Center, Woods Hole Laboratory, Lab. Ref. No. 80-10, November 1979.

Christy, F.T. "Distribution Systems for World Fisheries: Problems and Principles." *In Perspectives on Ocean Policy,* Conference on Ocean Relations, Airlie, Virginia, October 21-24, 1974.

Clark, S.H., and Essig, R.J. "Georges Bank and Gulf of Maine Haddock Assessment Update." National Marine Fisheries Service, Northeast Fisheries Center, Woods Hole Laboratory, Lab. Ref. No. 80-06, February 1980.

Clark, S.H.; Burns, T.S.; and Essig, R.J. "Scotian Shelf, Gulf of Maine, and Georges Bank Pollock Assessment Update." National Marine Fisheries Service, Northeast Fisheries Center, Woods Hole Laboratory, Lab. Ref. No. 79-59, December 1979.

Clark, S.H., and Overholtz, W.J. "Review and Assessment of the Georges Bank and Gulf of Maine Haddock Fishery." National Marine Fisheries Service, Northeast Fisheries Center, Woods Hole Laboratory, Lab. Ref. No. 79-05, January 1979.

Cohen, E.B.; Grosslein, M.D.; and Sissenwine, M.P. "An Energy Budget of Georges Bank." Presented at a workshop on multispecies approaches to fisheries management, St. John's, Newfoundland, November 26-30, 1979.

Cohen, E.B., and Wright, W.R. "Primary Productivity on Georges Bank with an Explanation of Why It Is So High." National Marine Fisheries Service, Northeast Fisheries Center, Woods Hole Laboratory, Lab. Ref. No. 79-53, November 1979.

Dirlam, S., ed. "New England-Canadiàn Maritime Provinces Fisheries Management Workshop Summary." Workshop held at University of Rhode Island, May 12-13, 1978.

Dunn, S.; McCorquodale, S.; and Pross, A.P. "East Coast Fisheries: Constitutional Issues in Newfoundland." Unpublished manuscript, Dalhousie University, 1981.

Greene, Stephen. "Washington: A Study of the U.S. Fish Policy Process." Halifax, Nova Scotia: Center for International Business Studies, Dalhousie University, 1978.

Hale, W., and Wittusen, D. "World Fisheries: A 'Tragedy of the Commons?'" Woodrow Wilson School of Public and International Affairs, Princeton, N.J., 1971.

Hare, G.M. "Atlas of the Major Atlantic Coast Fish and Invertebrate Resources Adjacent to the Canada-United States Boundary Areas." Environment Canada Fisheries and Marine Service Tech. Rept. No. 61, 1977.

Johnston, Douglas M. "The Administration of Canadian Fisheries." Unpublished manuscript, Dalhousie Law School, April 1978).

————. "Environmental Management in the South China Sea: Legal and Institutional Developments." East-West Environment and Policy Institute, Research Report No. 10: Honolulu, Hawaii, May 1982.

Knight, H. Gary, and Jackson, T. "Legal Impediments to the Use of Interstate Agreements in Co-ordinated Fisheries Management Programs: States in the N.M.F.S. Southeast Region." Louisiana State University, Office of Sea Grant Development, September 28, 1973.

Krouse, J.S. "Movement, Growth and Mortality of American Lobsters, Homarus americanus, Tagged along the Coast of Maine." NOAA Tech. Rept. NMFS SSRF-747, September 1981.

————. "Summary of Lobster, Homarus americanus, Tagging Studies in American Waters (1898-1978)." Can. Tech. Rep. Fish. Aquatic Sciences No. 932, pp. 135-140. Proceedings of the Canada-U.S. Workshop on Status of Assessment Science for the N.W. Atlantic Lobster (Homarus americanus) Stocks, March 1980.

Kulka, D.W., and Stobo, W.T. "Winter Distribution and Feeding of Mackerel on the Scotian Shelf and Outer Georges Bank with Reference to the Winter Distribution of Other Finfish Species." Canadian Tech. Rept. Fish. Aquatic Sciences No. 1038, (August 1981).

Lange, A. "Squid (Loligo pealei and Illex illecebrosus) Stock Status Update: July, 1979." National Marine Fisheries Service, Northeast Fisheries Center, Woods Hole Laboratory, Lab. Ref. No. 79-30, July 23, 1979.

Levelton, C.R. "Toward an Atlantic Coast Commercial Fisheries Licensing System." Report prepared for the Dept. of Fisheries and Oceans, Ottawa, Ontario, 1981.

Lough, R.G., and Bolz, G.R. "Abundance of Sea Herring (Clupea Harengus L.) Larval in Relation to Spawning Stock Size and Recruitment for the Gulf of Maine and Georges Bank, 1968-1978." National Marine Fisheries Service, Northeast Fisheries Center, Woods Hole Laboratory, Lab. Ref. No. 79-50, November 1979.

MacDonald, Doug, and Mazany, Leigh. "An Economic Analysis of Quality Improvement and Marketing Issues in the Atlantic Fishery." Prepared for the National Conference on the Future of the Atlantic Fisheries, June 3, 1982.

Mayo, R.K.; Bevacqua, E.; Gifford, W.M.; and Griffin, M.E. "An Assessment of the Gulf of Maine Redfish, Sebastes marinus (L.), Stock in 1978." National

Marine Fisheries Center, Northeast Fisheries Center, Woods Hole Laboratory, Lab. Ref. No. 79-20, May 1979.

Munroe, Cathy, and Stewart, Jim. "Fishermen's Organizations in Nova Scotia: The Potential for Unification." School of Business Administration, Dalhousie University, April 1981.

Pearse, Peter H. "Conflict and Opportunity: Toward a New Policy for Canada's Pacific Fisheries." Preliminary report of the Commission on Pacific Fisheries Policy, Vancouver, B.C., October 1981.

Pontecorvo, Giulio. "Fishery Management and the General Welfare: Implications of the New Structure." Research paper No. 157, Graduate School of Business, Columbia University, February 1977.

Rhode Island University. "Managing Our Georges Bank Resources," Proceedings from a workshop held at the W. Alton Jones Campus, University of Rhode Island, September 6-7, 1979, Kingston, Rhode Island.

Roger, C.F.E., and Lu, C.C. "Rhynchateauthion Larvae of Omastrephid Squids of the Western North Atlantic, with the First Description of Larvae and Juveniles of Illex illecebrosus." Fisheries and Marine Serv. Tech. Rept. No. 833, at 14:1, Proceedings of the Workshop on the Squid Illex illecebrosus, Dalhousie University, Halifax, Nova Scotia, May 1978.

Scott, Anthony, and Neher, Philip A., eds. "The Public Regulation of Commercial Fisheries in Canada." Ottawa: Supply and Services Canada, 1981.

Serchuck, F.M.; Wood, Jr., P.W.; and Freid, D.M. "Current Assessment and Status of the Georges Bank and Gulf of Maine Cod Stocks." National Marine Fisheries Service, Northeast Fisheries Center, Lab. Ref. No. 80-07, February 1980.

Sinclair, A.; Sinclair, M.; and Iles, T.D. "An Analysis of Some Biological Characteristics of the 4X Juvenile-Herring Fishery." Proceedings of the Nova Scotia Institute of Science, Vol. 31, Part 2, Halifax, Nova Scotia, 1981.

Sinclair, M., and Iles, T.D. "Adult Herring Feeding Area off S.W. Nova Scotia." Unpublished manuscript, Dept. of Fisheries and Oceans, Halifax, Nova Scotia, 1980.

Sinclair, M.; Iles, T.D.; and Sutcliffe, W. "Herring Distributions within the Scotian Shelf-Gulf of Maine Area in Relation to Oceangraphic Features." Paper presented to the Symposium on Biological Productivity of Continental Shelves in the Temperate Zone of the North Atlantic, Kiel, Germany, March 2-5, 1982.

Smith, M. Estellie. "The 'Public Face' of the New England Regional Fishery Council: Year 1." Woods Hole Oceanographic Institution, Tech. Rpt. 78-36, April 1978.

Stasko, A.B. "Tagging and Lobster Movements in Canada." Can. Tech. Rept. Fish. Aquatic Sciences No. 932, pp. 141-150, Proceedings of the Canada-U.S. Workshop on Status of Assessment Science for the N.W. Atlantic Lobster (Homarus americanus) Stocks, March 1980.

Stobo, W.T.; Moores, J.A.; and Maguire, J.J. "The Herring and Mackerel Resources on the East Coast." Background paper for the East Coast Herring and Mackerel Seminar, February 17-19, 1981.

Templeman, W. "Redfish Distribution in the North Atlantic." ICNAF Spec. Publ. No. 3, pp. 154-156, ICES/ICNAF Redfish Symposium, 1961.

Weeks, E.P. "Key Issues Facing the East Coast Fisheries of Canada." Dalhousie University, Center for Development Projects, December 1979.

Weeks, E.P., and Sommerville, A. "The Future of the Atlantic Fisheries." Institute for Research on Public Policy, Montreal, Quebec, 1981.

Theses

Beauchamp, Kenneth P. *The Management Function of Ocean Boundaries: Prospects For Co-operative Ocean Management Between Canada and the United States.* LL.M. thesis, Dalhousie Law School, 1981.

Jansen, J. *Regional Socio-Economic Development: The Case of Fishing in Atlantic Canada.* Ph.D. thesis, Rutgers University, 1981.

Redding, Forest William Jr. *Sharing the Living Resources of the Sea: An Analysis of Contemporary American-Canadian Fisheries Relations.* Ph.D. thesis, University of Oklahoma, 1979.

Schou, D. *International Law of the Sea: Some Determinants in U.S. Oceans Fishery Policy.* Ph.D. thesis, Florida State University, 1977.

Goverment Publications

Canada

Dept. Fisheries and Oceans. *Annual Report 1979-80.* 1981.

———. *Annual Report 1980-81.* 1982.

———. *Annual Report 1980, Maritimes Region.* 1981.

———. *Atlantic Groundfish Management Plan.* April 15, 1980.

———. *Canada's Atlantic Squid Fishery.* Fishermen's Information Bulletin. 1981.

———. *Canada's Department of Fisheries and Oceans.* 1981.

———. *Canada's Fishing Industry: A Sectoral Analysis.* March 1980.

———. *Canadian Atlantic Fisheries Scientific Advisory Committee (CAFSAC) Annual Report 1977-1978, Volume 1.* 1978.

———. *Canadian Atlantic Fisheries Scientific Advisory Committee (CAFSAC) Annual Report 1979, Volume II.* 1979.

———. *Canadian Fisheries Annual Statistical Review, Volume 12.* 1979.

_____. *Canadian Fisheries Policies and Objectives: A Briefing Session for the Diplomatic Community*. 1981.

_____. *Policy for Canada's Atlantic Fisheries in the 1980s*. 1981.

_____. *Resource Prospects for Canada's Atlantic Fisheries 1981–1987*. February 1981.

_____. *Sector Management of Canada's Atlantic Fisheries*. November 1981.

Economic Council of Canada. Reforming Regulation. Ottawa: Economic Council of Canada, 1981.

Environment Canada Fisheries and Marine Service. *The Atlantic Haddock*. Fisheries Fact Sheet No. 13. July 1974.

External Affairs Canada. *Statements and Speeches*, No. 80/22. Address by Honorable Mark MacGuigan to the Eleventh Leadership Conference of the Centre for the Study of the Presidency, Ottawa, Ontario. October 18, 1980.

Government of Canada. *The Canadian Constitution 1981*. Text of the Resolution respecting the Canadian Constitution adopted by the House of Commons on December 2, 1981, and by the Senate on December 8, 1981.

Province of Nova Scotia. *16th Annual Report, Department of Fisheries*. 1980.

United States

Comptroller General of the United States. *Progress and Problems of Fisheries Management under the Fishery Conservation and Management Act*. January 9, 1979.

Hearings before the Subcommittee on International Security and Scientific Affairs of the Committee on International Relations. House of Representatives. 94th Cong., 2d sess., June 22, 23, 29, 30, July 20, 22, 1976. Washington, D.C.: U.S. Government Printing Office.

Hearings on Senate Resolution 486 Relating to the Treaty Powers of the Senate, before the Committee on Foreign Relations United States Senate, 94th Cong., 2d sess., July 21, 28, 1976, Washington, D.C.: U.S. Government Printing Office.

Hearing on the Fishery Conservation and Management Act of 1976, before the Senate Committee on Commerce, Science and Transportation, 95th Cong., 2d sess., January 9, 1978. Washington, D.C.: U.S. Government Printing Office.

Hearings on Fishery Conservation and Management Act Oversight, before the House Subcommittee on Fisheries and Wildlife Conservation and the Environment of the Committee on Merchant Marine and Fisheries. 96th Cong., 1st sess., 1979. Washington, D.C.: U.S. Government Printing Office.

Hearings on United States-Canadian Fishing Agreements, before the House Subcommittee on Fisheries and Wildlife Conservation and the Environment of the Committee on Merchant Marine and Fisheries. 96th Cong., 1st sess., June 22, 1979. Washington, D.C.: U.S. Government Printing Office.

Hearings on Commercial Fisheries Authorization and Oversight—H.R. 4890, before the Subcommittee on Fisheries and Wildlife Conservation and the Environment and Oceanography of the House Committee on Merchant Marine and Fisheries. 96th Cong., 2d sess. (February 11, 1980). Washington, D.C.: U.S. Government Printing Office.

Hearing on the Maritime Boundary Settlement Treaty with Canada, before the Senate Committee on Foreign Relations. 97th Cong., 1st sess. March 18, 1981. Washington, D.C.: U.S. Government Printing Office.

Mid-Atlantic Fishery Management Council. *Final Environmental Impact Statement/Fishery Management Plan for the Squid Fishery of the Northwest Atlantic Ocean.* April 1978.

New England Fishery Management Council. *Fishery Management Plan, Final Environmental Impact Statement, Regulatory Impact Review for Atlantic Sea Scallops (Placopecten magellanicus).* January, 1982.

———. *Interim Fishery Management Plan for Atlantic Groundfish.* September 30, 1981.

National Marine Fisheries Service. *Summary of Stock Assessment.* Northeast Fisheries Center, Woods Hole Laboratory, Lab. Ref. No. 79–41. September 1979.

———. *A Short Run Economic Impact Analysis of the U.S.-Canadian Agreement on East Coast Fishery Resources.* October 1979.

Office of Technology Assessment. *Establishing a 200-Mile Fisheries Zone.* 1977.

Senate Committee on Commerce and National Ocean Policy Study. 94th Cong., 2d sess. *A Legislative History of the Fishery Conservation and Management Act of 1976.* 1976.

U.S. Dept. Commerce. *Calendar Year 1979 Report on the Implementation of the Magnuson Fishery and Conservation Act of 1976.* March 1980.

———. *Calendar Year 1980 Report on the Implementation of the Magnuson Fishery and Conservation Act of 1976.* March 1981.

———. *Fisheries of the United States, 1980.* April 1981.

———. *Fishery Conservation and Management Act Operations Handbook.* October 1980.

———. *U.S. Ocean Policy in the 1970s: Status and Issues.* 1978.

U.S. Dept. Interior. Bureau of Land Management. *Final Environmental Statement, Proposed 1977 Outer Continental Shelf Oil & Gas Lease Sale Offshore the North Atlantic States, OCS Sale No. 42.* 1977.

U.S. Dept. State. *Background and Analysis: East Coast Maritime Boundary and Fisheries Treaties with Canada.* March 28, 1979.

———. 11 *Foreign Affairs Manual* 721.2. October 25, 1974.

———. *Draft Environmental Impact Statement on the Agreement Between the United States and Canada on East Coast Fishery Resources.* April 1980.

———. *Draft Environmental Impact Statement on the Agreement between the United States and Canada on East Coast Fisheries Resources, Appendices.* March 1980.

_____. *United States-Canada East Coast Fishery Resources Agreement Data Summary*. 1978.

United Nations Documents

Draft Convention on the Law of the Sea. U.N. Doc. A/CONF. 62/L. 78. August 28, 1981.

U.N. Conference on the Law of Treaties. U.N. Doc. A/CONF. 39/27. May 23, 1969.

U.N. Resolution on Co-operation in the Field of the Environment Concerning Natural Resources Shared by Two or More States. U.N. Doc. A/34/186. December 18, 1981.

Report of the Intergovernmental Working Group of Experts on Natural Resources Shared by Two or More States on the Work of Its Fifth Session Held at Nairobi from January 23 to February 7, 1978, UNEP GC. 6/17. *Reprinted* in 17 Int'l Legal Materials 1094-1099.

Index

American Fisheries Defense Committee, 90, 91
Arctic, 67
Argentine, 14–15, 25, 26 fn 15, 93, fn 4
Atlantic Groundfish Advisory Committee, 72, 74, 100
Atlantic Groundfish Management Plan (Canada), 72–75. *See also* Canada, administration of fisheries
Atlantic States Marine Fisheries Commission, 43, 57 fn 64, 62 fn 99

British Columbia, 64, 65, 80 fn 16, 81 fn 18

Campbell, Tony, 96, 99
Canada, 3, 5, 9, 25, 28 fn 37, 29 fn 47, 55 fn 40, 56 fn 59, 59 fn 76, 89, 91, 93 fn 6, 95, 96, 97, 98, 99, 100, 101, 103, 104, 105, 106, 107 fn 3; administration of fisheries, 66–67, 69–72, 73; and foreign fishing, 67, 68, 69, 74, 76, 82 fn 30, 84 fn 51; federal-provincial disputes, 63–66; fish export, 28 fn 38, 29 fn 48, 29 fn 60, 87 fn 78; fish landing statistics, 5, 6–7, 8–9, 10, 12–13, 15–19, 21, 23–24, 31 fn 82; fisheries legislation, 68–69; international jurisdiction, 67–68; problems with the fishery, 76–79. *See also* Atlantic Groundfish Management Plan; Department of Fisheries and Oceans
Canada Atlantic Fisheries Scientific Advisory Committee (CAFSAC), 72, 75, 85 fn 55
Cadieux, Marcel, 89
Carter, President Jimmy, 90, 110 fn 30
Cod, 1, 5, 25, 26 fn 15, 28 fn 37, 48, 50, 84 fn 51, 89, 93 fn 4, 93 fn 5,

100; distribution of, 5–6; management of, 28 fn 37; statistics, 6–7
Commerce Department (U.S.), 39, 40, 43, 44, 45, 46, 47, 49, 54 fn 28, 101, 105
Commission on Pacific Fisheries Policy (Canada), 86 fn 58
Connecticut, 39, 57 fn 62, 57 fn 64
Convention on the Law of the Sea, 29 fn 61, 46, 57 fn 59, 108 fn 15. *See also* United Nations Conference on the Law of the Sea (UNCLOS III)
Cusk, 15–16, 25, 26 fn 15, 92 fn 3
Cutler, Lloyd, 89

Department of Commerce (U.S.). *See* Commerce Department (U.S.)
Department of Fisheries and Oceans (Canada), 68, 69, 77, 78, 79, 83 fn 38, 83 fn 42, 83 fn 43, 101, 105; organization of, 69–72; origins, 66–67; responsibilities, 67; role in fisheries management, 72–76

East Coast Fisheries Agreement, 1979, 3, 72, 95, 96, 97, 109 fn 23; and fish allocations, 89, 91, 97–98; U.S. problems with, 90–92, 97–101
Executive agreements (U.S.), 96, 101–105

Federal-Provincial Atlantic Fisheries Committee (Canada), 74
Fisheries Act (Canada), 63, 64, 68
Fishery Conservation and Management Act (FCMA) (U.S.), 39, 40, 41, 42, 47, 56 fn 52, 62 fn 99, 91; and foreign fleets, 42–43; enforcement, 49–50; fisheries management, 43, 44–46
Flounder, 1, 28 fn 37, 48, 50, 100

About the Author

David L. VanderZwaag is currently a full-time researcher with the Dalhousie Ocean Studies Programme. He received the B.A. from Calvin College, the M.Div. from Princeton Theological Seminary, the J.D. from the University of Arkansas, and the LL.M. in the law of the sea from Dalhousie University.